This Text Book is useful for Sir Parashurambhau College of Arts, Science and Commerce, Pune. (Autonomous)

## Economics (G-2)

# Modern Banking - II

### S.Y. B. A. (Sem. - IV) (Course Code : EC2416)

**Dr. Nasir Shaikh**
(M.A. (Eco), M.Phil. (Eco), M.M.S. (Mkt), M.Ed., Ph.D.)
Marathwada Mitra Mandal College of Commerce, Pune.

**Df. Archana Aher**
(M.A., M.Phil., B.Ed., M.Ed., L.L.B., SET, Ph.D.
MIT Arts, Commerce & Science College, Alandi, Pune.



2023

Price: 110/-

SUCCESS PUBLICATIONS

*Published by*
*Dr. Rajesh M. Patne*
**Success Publications**
Radha Krishna Apartment, 535, Shaniwar Peth,
Appa Balwant Chowk, Opp. Prabhat Talkies, Pune - 411 030.
Ph. 24434662 Mobile : 9325315464.



*Printed at*
**Success Publications**
S. No. 30/27, Laxmi Industrial Estate,
Near Prabhat News Paper, Dhayari, Pune-41.

*Edition*
2023

*Edited By*
Mr. Valmik Gaikwad

*Typesetting, Layout*
Mr. Valmik Gaikwad

*Cover Designing*
Miss. Varsha Lokhande

***ISBN NO. – 978-93-93220-55-4***

# Preface

*It is a matter of great pleasure for us to present this book to our esteemed readers. This book has been designed as standard text on 'Financial System – II' for S.Y.B.A. (Sem. - IV).*

*This book comprehensively covers the entire syllabus of S.Y.B.A. (Sem. - IV) Course of Sir Parashurambhau College (Autonomous), Pune effective from 2020 onwards. It has been written to meet the requirements of students of S.Y.B.A. (Sem. - II) Some of the special features of the book are as follows:*

**1.** *Full coverage of the revised syllabus of S.Y.B.A. (Sem. - IV).*

**2.** *Chapter outline at the beginning of each chapter to give a bird's eye view of the topics covered in the chapter.*

**3.** *Point wise explanation of each topic in the chapter.*

**4.** *Topics are logically arranged in numbered paragraphs exactly according to the modified syllabus.*

**5.** *Proposed questions at the end of each chapter.*

**6.** *Extensive use of diagrams, tables and various forms to give visual view of key concepts and techniques.*

**7.** *Conversational, lucid and simple language.*

*Every effort has been made to provide the readers with most up-to-date and authentic material on the subject.*

*We are very grateful to our publisher Mrs. and Mr. Rajesh Patne who have rendered all possible assistance in bringing out this book. We wish to acknowledge our deep gratitude to staff who have assisted and helped us in preparing this book. We will consider our efforts amply rewarded in case the book proves useful to the students and teachers of the subject.*

*Suggestions of readers are welcome and shall be acknowledged with gratitude.*

***With best wishes.***

***By Authors***

# Syllabus

**S. Y. B.A. (Sem. - IV)**

**Economics G-2 (Modern Banking - II) (Course Code – EC2416)**

| Unit No. | Unit Title & Contents | No. of Lectures |
|---|---|---|
| 1 | **Co-operative Banking in India** | 12 |
| | • Principles of Cooperation<br>• Meaning and significance of co-operative banking in India<br>• Evolution and structure of Cooperative Banks in India.<br>• Role of Co-operative Banks in Rural Development<br>• Performance and Challenges before Co-operative Banks in India | |
| 2 | **Development Banks in India** | 10 |
| | • Meaning and Features of Development Banks<br>• Functions of Development Banks in India<br>• Role of Development Banks in Economic Development<br>• Challenges before the Development Banking in India | |
| 3 | **Banking Sector Reforms** | 16 |
| | • Meaning and Goals of Banking Sector Reforms in India<br>• Recommendations of M. Narsimham Committee I (1991)<br>• Recommendations of M. Narsimham Committee II (1998)<br>• Banking Reform Measures:<br>○ Cash Reserve Ratio (C.R.R.) and Statutory Liquidity Ratio (S.L.R.)<br>○ Credit-Deposit Ratio (C. D. R.)<br>○ Basel norms- I, II, III, IV | |
| 4 | **Innovative Banking in India** | 10 |
| | • MUDRA Scheme - Objectives & Salient<br>• Features of MUDRA Loan Scheme<br>• Small Finance Banks - Organization, Functions & Importance<br>• Payment Banks Organization, Functions & Importance<br>• Bandhan Bank | |

# INDEX

**S. Y. B.A. (Sem. - IV)**

**Economics G-2 (Modern Banking - II) (Course Code – EC2416)**


| Unit | Topic | Page No. |
|---|---|---|
| 1 | **Co-operative Banking in India** | 1.1 to 1.21 |
| | **1.1** Co-operation<br>**1.2** Co-operative Banking in India<br>**1.3** Structure of Co-operative Banking in India<br>**1.4** Role of Co-operative Banks in Economic Development<br>**1.5** Performance of Co-operative Banking in India<br>**1.6** Challenges before Co-operative Banking in India | |
| 2 | **Development Banks in India** | 2.1 to 2.12 |
| | **2.1** Concept of Development Banking<br>**2.2** Features of Development Banking<br>**2.3** Functions of Development Banks<br>**2.4** Role of Development Banks in Economic Development<br>**2.5** Challenges before Development Banking in India | |
| 3 | **Banking Sector Reforms** | 3.1 to 3.31 |
| | **3.1** Banking Sector Reforms in India<br>**3.2** Narsimhan Committee – I<br>**3.3** Narsimhan Committee – II<br>**3.4** Banking Reforms Measures<br>**3.5** Framework of Basel Committees on Banking Supervision | |
| 4. | **Innovative Banking in India** | 4.1 to 4.17 |
| | **4.1** MUDRA Scheme<br>**4.2** Small Finance Banks<br>**4.3** Payment Banks<br>**4.4** Bandhan Bank | |

UNIT 1

# Co-operative Banking in India

**1.1 Co-operation**

**1.2 Co-operative Banking in India**

**1.3 Structure of Co-operative Banking in India**

**1.4 Role of Co-operative Banks in Economic Development**

**1.5 Performance of Co-operative Banking in India**

**1.6 Challenges before Co-operative Banking in India**

## Introduction:

Cooperative movement in India was started primarily for dealing with the problem of rural credit. The history of Indian cooperative banking started with the passing of Cooperative Societies Act in 1904. The objective of this Act was to establish cooperative credit societies "to encourage thrift, self-help and cooperation among agriculturists, artisans and persons of limited means." There are different types of cooperative credit institutions working in India. These institutions can be classified into two broad categories- agricultural and non-agricultural. Agricultural credit institutions dominate the entire cooperative credit structure. Cooperative Banking and Credit Institutions play an important role in meeting the growing credit needs of India. Many economically weak persons come together for achieving the common objective and form the co-operative society. Through this society they solve their mutual difficulties, help each other and fulfill their objectives. There are various kinds of co-operative societies and they have various objectives. The volume of credit flowing through these institutions has increased. The performance of these institutions, however, has been less than satisfactory and is deteriorating rapidly.

## 1.1 Co-operation:

Co-operation is the cornerstone of social development, no matter where in the world. People create societies through co-operation, and no actor can manage this process on their own. They can only achieve this through good co-operation relationships at the local level, within entire societies and increasingly across national borders. The days when only states and governments co-operated with each other are long gone. Civil society and private sector actors are now also joining co-operation systems. Co-operation means working with others on a common task. Co-operative people work together to reach goals. Big tasks seem smaller when each person does one part of the task. A group often can reach a goal that one person cannot. The term co-operation, thus, connotes several meanings and it is difficult to convey the correct meaning of co-operation, in its technical sense. Its meaning has varied from thinker to thinker and from one sphere of human activity to the other.

### 1.1.1 Meaning:

Co-operation is derived from the Latin word "Co-operari", 'Co' means "with" and 'operari' means "to work". Hence co-operation means Working Together with others for a common purpose. Aristotle, a Philosopher of Ancient Greece, recognised the social nature of man when he said, "Man is a Social Animal". Man cannot lead a happy and contented life if he lives in isolation. Therefore, there is a great need for Co-operation, which can be considered as the basic principle underlying human life. The basic idea behind Co-operation is "Self Help and Mutual Help" and "Mutual Aid" and "Each for all and all for each".

### 1.1.2 Definitions:

Following are the Definitions of Co-operation:

1) **Dr. Mladenatz :**
   *"Co-operative enterprises are associations of persons, small producers or consumers who come together voluntarily to achieve some purpose by reciprocal exchange of service, through an economic enterprise working at their own risk and with resources to which all contribute."*
2) **Mr. Watkins :**
   *"Co-operation as system of social organisation based on the principles of unity, economy, democracy, equity and liberty."*
3) **Anotoine Antoni :**
   *"A cooperative is an association of persons pursuing aims of social, economic and educational character and forming for their attainment an enterprise which operates in accordance with the principles of democracy and collective ownership."*
4) **Dr. E.M. Hough :**
   *"Co-operation may be defined simply as voluntary association in a joint undertaking for mutual benefit"*

**5) Seligman:**

*"Co-operation in its technical sense means the abandonment of competition in distribution and production and the elimination of middlemen of all kinds."*

## 1.1.3 Principles of Co-operation:

The co-operative principles are guidelines for co-operative organisations. The main principles of co-operation are given below:

**1) Voluntary and Open Membership:**

The vital principle of co-operation is voluntary and open membership of co-operative organisation. Membership is open to all, irrespective of religion, caste creed, region or race. The co-operative organisation is a voluntary form of organisation. There is no compulsion on anybody to join the society or to resign it.

**2) Autonomy and Independence:**

Co-operative organisations/societies are autonomous and independent units. These organisations are controlled by their members. The members elect their representative on Board of Director. Such Board is responsible for direction and control of management of the society within the policy laid down by general body. The members can amend the bye-laws and carry out the society's activity. Thus, every co-operative has got full autonomy and it is also an independent unit from external forces. It can raise fund from the government through proper agreement.

**3) Democratic Control:**

Democratic member control is fundamental principle of co-operation. A society/ organisation are managed on a one member - one vote basis. The voting right is not based or determined on number of shares held by the member. Thus, due to democratic form of co-operative organisation all members have equal right and opportunity to participate in the conduct of its affairs.

**4) Co-operation among Co-operatives:**

This principle is considered as the principle of growth and development in co-operation among co-operatives. It means that every co-operative is helping the remaining co-operatives. For example, credit co-operative are helping to marketing co-operatives, processing co-operatives consumer co-operatives and other co-operatives. In this way, they can strengthen the co-operative movement at local, national and international level too. Thus, inter-relationship exists among these co-operatives in respect with financial and business as well as vertical and horizontal structure.

**5) Members' Economic Participation:**

Members of the organisation / society contribute equally. It is a common property of the society. In every economic activity they participate actively. The members can allocate their surplus funds for development purpose. They get interest for their capital and also dividends. Sometimes they get rebate on purchases of building etc. Thus, every member's economic participation is allowed. The undistributed profit goes to the reserve fund.

**6) Concern for Community:**

Co-operative helps for sustained development and welfare of the community through policies approved by their members.

**7) Education, Training and Information:**

Co-operative provides education, training and information about co-operative for their members, to their managers, employees and elected representatives. As result of this, they will contribute effectively to the development of their co-operatives. The educated and trained people may inform the public, the importance and usefulness of co-operatives.

**8) Cash Trading:**

Japan, India, Srilanka, Sweden, etc. are upholding cash trading as more principle than a policy guideline. Cash trading are developing self-respect and reducing the risk of bad debts. Cash trading is good for the mental health and physical health of the member of the society.

**9) Self - Help through Mutual Help:**

Co-operative is working together for mutual benefit. It stands for self - help through mutual help. Its sole purpose is the common action for the common good and not for the individuals only.

**10) Political and Religious Neutrality:**

The principle of political and religious neutrality means absence of discriminations on the basis of religion and politics among the members. The co-operatives grant the full freedom to their members to have any religion. In other words, the society is neutral over the issues of politics and religion. The fall of these principles is achieved through:

**i)** Admitting all the persons regardless of politics, creed, nationality, race, colour, class or even sex.

**ii)** Refusing to serve a particular interest of political or religious groups.

**iii)** Keeping the individual's independence in fact.

**11) Equity, Unity and Fraternity:**

The principle of equity, unity and fraternity means two things viz. equity and justice on one hand and unity and fraternity on the other hand. The concept of equity and justice is originated as a reaction against injustice of capitalism.

The principle of unity and fraternity speaks about the great philosophy of universal brotherhood. As a result of this, nobody will be exploited in the co-operative society.

**12) Honorary Services:**

The co-operatives are designed to serve the economic and social interest of its members. The principle of service orientation speaks about the service about profit.

The concept of service motive should not be confused with extension of honorary service to the society by the members. As the earlier co-operative societies were small having a humble beginning, they should have such members to nurture, guide, supervise and manage the society without any remuneration.

**13) Publicity and Propaganda:**

This principle emphasises the fact that the society should develop with the help of publicity and propaganda. In the context of publicity, it is an effort to make available certain information to the public. As a result of publicity, people and members of the society can understand the importance of co-operative movement and society.

## 1.2 Co-operative Banking in India:

Cooperative banking is retail and commercial banking organized on a cooperative basis. Cooperative banking institutions take deposits and lend money in most parts of the world. Cooperative banking, as discussed here, includes retail banking carried out by credit unions, mutual savings banks, building societies and cooperatives, as well as commercial banking services provided by mutual organizations (such as cooperative federations) to cooperative businesses.

### 1.2.1 Meaning:

Co-Operative Banks are small financial institutions that offer lending facilities to small businesses in both urban and non-urban regions. These are monitored and regulated by the Reserve Bank of India (RBI) and come under the Banking Regulations Act, 1949 as well as the banking laws act, 1965.

Co-operative banks are financial entities established on a co-operative basis and belonging to their members. This means that the customers of a co-operative bank are also its owners. These banks provide a wide range of regular banking and financial services. However, there are some points where they differ from other banks.

### 1.2.2 Significance of Co-operative Banking:

In the agro-based developing economy like India, importance of co-operative banking is as follows:

**1) A Ray of the Hope :**

When the socially weak and helpless persons come together on the principle of equality and try to raise their financial level by helping each other, they set up a co-operative institution. In case of a poor country like India more than 65 percent people live on agriculture and they are stricken by poverty, ignorance and exploitation. Therefore, for eradication of their poverty and unemployment and miserable life co-operative movement is a ray of hope.

**2) Encouragement to Savings :**

Co-operative banks create habits of economy and savings among their members. Similarly, they impart education of banking transactions. Co-operative banks meet the economic needs of the general public at the local level. The important function of co-operative banks is to raise the level of savings of the general public.

**3) Supply of Credit :**

Near about 74% population lives in villages and agriculture is the main occupation of this population. Small, medium and big farmers require short term, medium term and long term loans. Co-operative banks and credit societies play a vital role in making the availability of the supply of credits to these people.

**4) Improvement in the Standard of Living :**

As co-operative banks provide loans to agriculture, the loans contribute to increase production, productivity of agriculture and incomes of the class of farmers. Due to rise in income of the common farmers, their standard of living improves.

**5) Freedom from the Clutches of Money Lenders :**

Before existence of co-operative banks, farmers were provided credits by the class of money lenders, merchants and landlords. In the year 1951, nearly 93 percent of loans were supplied by the private sources. Today also this proportion is 42 percent. Money lenders and landlords make cruel exploitation of farmers while supplying loans to them. If there is spreading of area of operations of co-operative banks far and wide, it will help the poor farmers to get rid of clutches of money lenders.

**6) Inducement to Rural Development :**

Co-operative banks under take different activities for rural development in addition to their credit supply to farmers. Co-operative banks supply loans at the concessional rate of interest and in easy installments to economically and socially weak sections of population to whom commercial banks do not give financial assistance. This leads to inducement to productive activities. So, productive investment is induced and the rural development gets direction in a proper way with the development of farmers.

**7) National Benefits :**

Co-operative banks perform banking business in the rural area. So, people in villages form habit of savings and investments. New progressive approach is created in the rural area. This ultimately gives benefit to people and the whole nation.

**8) Instrument of Economic Change :**

Co-operative banks in underdeveloped economy not only do the function of the acceptance of deposits and supply of credit. They also impart education of conducting democratic institutions through their working. The co-operative banks play the role of the economic and social change.

### 1.2.3 Evolution of Co-operative Banking:

This provides a brief review of the various phases of the evolution of cooperatives in general, and of credit cooperatives in particular, over the past century.

1) **The First Phase: 1900-1930:**

By the beginning of the 20th Century, officials of the colonial government perceived the Indian farmers' dependence on usurious moneylenders to be a major cause of their indebtedness and poverty. At that time the cooperative movement had become well established in Europe and achieved remarkable success there. Convinced that the cooperative movement offered the best means of liberating Indian farmers from the crushing burden of debt and the tyranny of moneylenders, Indian officials began to take active interest in promoting credit cooperatives in the country. Societies were organised for the first time in the closing years of the 19th Century.

The passage of the Cooperative Credit Societies Act in 1904, and the enactment of a more comprehensive Cooperative Societies Act in 1912 marked the beginning of a government policy of active encouragement and promotion of cooperatives. This thinking gained wide acceptance and was adopted as a policy by provincial governments and thereafter, "cooperation" became a provincial subject in 1919. The persistence of government interest in cooperatives and the importance attached to them was reflected in the appointment of three different Committees to review their growth and functioning.

The classic study by Frederic Nicholson, followed by the Edward Law Committee on Cooperative Legislation, confirmed and reiterated the need for the State to actively promote cooperatives. A decade later, the Maclagan Committee (1915) advocated that "there should be one cooperative for every village and every village should be covered by a cooperative". The Royal Commission on Agriculture in India, which submitted its report in 1928, suggested among other things, that the cooperative movement should continue to focus on expanding rural credit and that the State should patronise cooperatives and protect the sector.

It was the Royal Commission which made the observation "if cooperation fails, there will fail the best hope of rural India". By this time, the State was already deeply involved in promoting agricultural credit cooperatives. The number of societies reached impressive proportions and diversified their activities well beyond agricultural credit. Debates centred on whether or not each village should have a cooperative and whether there should be a single purpose or a multipurpose cooperative at the village level.

2) **The Second Phase: 1930-1950:**

The major development during this phase was the role played by the Reserve Bank of India (RBI). The Reserve Bank's concern and involvement in the sphere of rural credit stemmed from its very statute of incorporation. Specific provisions were made in the Reserve Bank of India Act, 1934 both for the establishment of an Agricultural Credit Department (ACD) in the bank and for extending refinance facilities to the cooperative credit system. Emphasis was laid on setting up, strengthening and promoting financially viable provincial cooperative banks, central cooperative banks, marketing societies and primary agricultural credit societies in each province. The RBI, since 1942, also started extending credit facilities to provincial cooperative banks for seasonal agricultural operations and marketing of crops.

The Government policy during this phase was not as pro-active on promoting cooperatives as before. There seemed to be a policy lull until 1945, when the Agricultural Finance Sub-committee and the Cooperative Planning Committee were set up by the Government of India (GoI). By then, there already were signs of sickness in the Indian rural cooperative movement. A large number of cooperatives were found to be saddled with the problem of frozen assets, because of heavy over dues in repayment. The Sub-committee's recommendation that the frozen assets of the members of such cooperatives be liquidated, by adjusting the claims of the society to the repaying capacity of the members, marked the beginning of State interference in the management of cooperatives and the consequent erosion in the credit discipline of the members. The Cooperative Planning Committee identified the small size of the primary cooperative as the principal cause of failure. It also advocated State protection to the cooperative sector from competition.

**3) The Third Phase: 1950-1990:**

After Independence, rapid and equitable economic development became the central focus of State policy. Cooperatives in general and rural financial cooperatives in particular, were once again on centre stage. Taking cognisance of the weakness of the cooperative system, the All India Rural Credit Survey (AIRCS) not only recommended State partnership in terms of equity, but also partnership in terms of governance and management. Other recommendations included linking credit and marketing cooperatives and enlarging their area of operation. The recommendations of the AIRCS stopped just short of the Government running the cooperatives, and paved the way for its direct intrusion in the governance and management of cooperatives.

State policy came to be premised on the view that the government should ensure adequate supply of cheap institutional credit to rural areas through cooperatives. The thinking then was that if the institutions that were meant to deliver such cheap institutional credit failed, there either had to be reorganisation of existing institutions, or creation of new types of institutions. The Hazari Committee recommended integration of short term and long term structures. The Bawa Committee (1971) recommended setting up Large Multi-purpose Cooperatives in tribal areas. The National Commission on Agriculture (1976) recommended setting up Farmers Service Cooperative Societies with the active collaboration of the nationalised banks.

NABARD was created on the recommendation of the CRAFICARD (Sivaraman Committee 1981). The State's heightened interest in and concern for the performance of cooperatives in the country was obvious. The focus, however, was on expanding and reorganising the State supported structures, without addressing the tasks of restoring and strengthening autonomy, mutual help and self-governance that are the cornerstones of genuine cooperatives.

The State gave primacy to cooperatives as the sole means of delivering institutional credit to rural areas and injected large and increasing amounts of funds directly. Upper tier cooperative banks were encouraged to accept public deposits and borrow from other financial institutions. However, the system was soon found to be burdened by growing overdues. In keeping with the national priority of financing the rural sector adequately, the involvement of commercial banks was first suggested as a social control measure. The involvement of commercial banks was thereafter institutionalized through the nationalisation of major commercial banks in 1969. During the post-nationalisation period, there was an unprecedented penetration of commercial banks in the rural sector. This trend, however, was accompanied by rigid policy directives right down to the micro level on cost of credit, purposes, categories of borrowers, geographical areas, etc.

As the financial involvement of the government in cooperatives increased, its interference in all aspects of the functioning of cooperatives also increased. The consequent interference with the functioning of the co-operative institutions, often compelling them to compromise on the usual norms for credit worthiness, ultimately began to affect the quality of the portfolio of the cooperatives.

The State has used co-operatives to channel its development schemes, particularly subsidy-based programmes for the poor. As these institutions have a wide reach in the rural areas and also deal with finances, the choice was natural. The trend, however, also made cooperatives a conduit for distributing political patronage. This and the sheer magnitude of resources and benefits channeled through the societies, makes control of decision-making and management attractive to parties in power, for accommodating their members, to influence decisions through directives, and for individual politicians to be on the management boards of the cooperatives.

**4) The Fourth Phase: 1990s and onwards:**

During the last fifteen years, there has been an increasing realisation of the destructive effects of intrusive State patronage, politicisation, and the consequent impairment of the role of cooperatives in general, and of credit cooperatives in particular, leading to a quest for reviving and revitalising the cooperative movement. Several Committees were set up to suggest cooperative sector reforms during this period. Progress in implementing these suggestions has been very tardy because of the States' unwillingness to share in costs and their reluctance to dilute their powers and to cede regulatory powers to the Reserve Bank of India (RBI). The passage of the Mutually Aided Cooperative Societies Act by the Andhra Pradesh government in 1995, however, marked a significant step towards reform. Following the example of Andhra Pradesh, eight other States (viz., Bihar, Chhattisgarh, Jammu and Kashmir, Jharkhand, Karnataka, Madhya Pradesh, Orissa and Uttaranchal) have passed similar legislation to govern and regulate mutually aided cooperatives.

In all cases these new laws provide for cooperatives to be democratic, self-reliant and member-centric, without any State involvement or financial support. They provide for cooperatives registered under the old law to migrate to the new Act. The old Acts were not repealed, nor was there any serious effort to encourage and facilitate the conversion of old cooperatives to come within the purview of the new Act. Most existing cooperatives, therefore, continued to adhere to the old law.

The new law, however, did lead to the emergence of a "new generation autonomous financial cooperatives", albeit slowly and unevenly across the country. While the number of cooperatives registered under the new liberal Act is slowly picking up, the conversion from the old law to the new Act has largely been in the arena of commodity cooperatives. The reason for the slow pace at which both credit cooperatives and the primary agricultural credit societies (PACS) are adopting the new law is largely because they are not eligible for refinance under the existing legal and structural arrangements.

## 1.3 Structure of Co-operative Banking in India:

The co-operative banking system is the integral part of the Indian Financial system. The co-operative banking system includes the Urban and Rural co-operative institutions. These co-operative institutions have performed the important developmental role through their wide network and the branches spreading far and wide in case of creation of banking habits among the people. The structure of co-operative banking has developed and is developing for more than 50 years.

Broadly, co-operative banks in India are divided into two categories - urban and rural. Rural cooperative credit institutions could either be short-term or long-term in nature. Further, short-term cooperative credit institutions are further sub-divided into State Co-operative Banks, District Central Co-operative Banks, Primary Agricultural Credit Societies. Meanwhile, the long-term institutions are either State Cooperative Agriculture or Rural Development Banks (SCARDBs) or Primary Cooperative Agriculture and Rural Development Banks (PCARDBs).

On the other hand, Urban Co-operative Banks (UBBs) are either scheduled or non-scheduled. Scheduled and non-scheduled UCBs are again of two kinds- multi-state and those operating in single state.

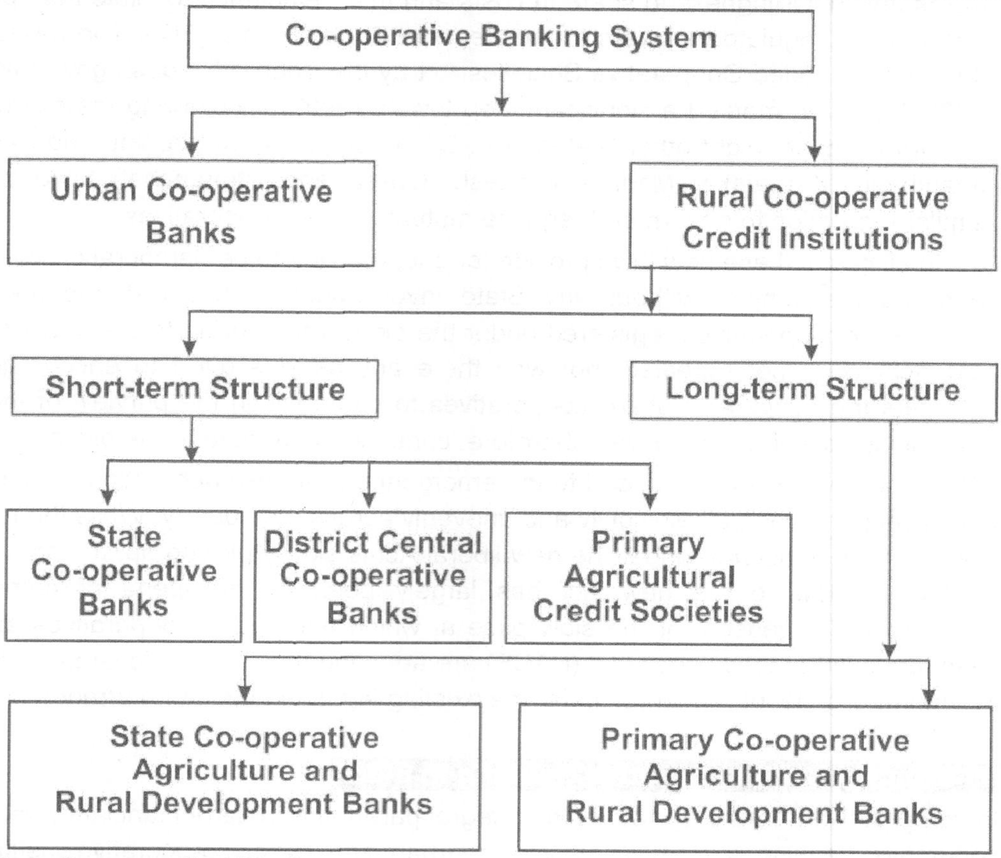


**1) Urban Co-operative Banks:**

The structure of Urban Co-operative Banking is of single tier system. This is called the Primary Co-operative Banks. These banks function in non-agricultural sector. These banks make facilities available to citizens, small traders and merchants and small scale industries belonging to small income group in the urban sector. At the end of March 2004, 2105 urban co-operative banks with their 8,166 branches were existing in India.

**2) Rural Co-operative Credit Institutions:**

Rural co-operative credit societies function in agricultural sector. The structure of these societies is divided between:

**a) Short-term Structure:**

The structure of short-term co-operative credit institutions is of three-tier system.

1) State Co-operative Bank at the state level.
2) District Central Co-operative Bank at the district level.
3) Primary agricultural credit societies at the village level. The primary agricultural credit society is only the institution and not a bank.

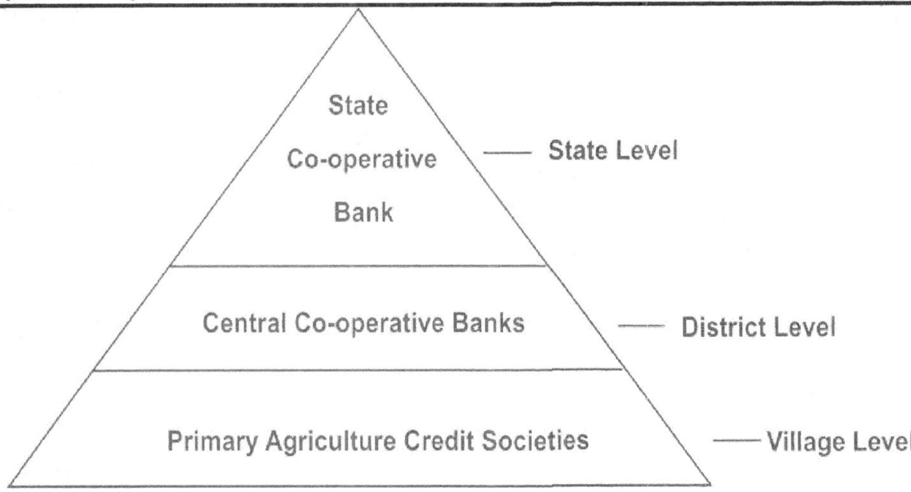


**A) State Co-operative Banks:**

Generally, there is one State Co-operative Bank in each state. The main functions of these banks are to supervise the working of Central Co-operative Banks, to advice and to guide them and to provide finance to them. These banks are known as "Apex bank" in the respective state. These banks obtain loans from the Reserve Bank of India, State Bank of India, etc. and these loans are given to primary agricultural credit societies through the District Central Banks. At the end of March 2003, number of state co-operative Banks were 30.

**B) The District Central Co-operative Banks:**

The District Central co-operative Banks function at the district level. All the Primary Agricultural Credit Societies (PACS) are the members of the District Central Co-operative Bank in the respective state. Some District Central Co-operative Banks allow membership to private individuals also. These banks provide finance to primary agricultural credit societies, supervise them, control them, etc. At the end of March 2003, the number of the District Central Co-operative Banks was 367.

**C) Primary Agricultural Credit Societies:**

Primary Agricultural credit society's work at the local level. Generally, each village has a single primary agricultural credit society. These societies provide finance to agriculture, cottage industries, etc. A village in which a primary agricultural credit society is set up, people in that village can become members of that society. This society functions only for that village. The society uses its share capital, deposits and loans taken from the District Central Co-operative Bank for providing finance to borrowers. At the end of $31^{st}$ March 2003, the total number of primary agricultural credit societies were 1, 12,309 and the number of members were 120 million.

**b) Long-Term Structure:**

Long-term co-operative credit structure is normally of two-tier system.

1) **State Co-operative Agriculture and Rural Development Banks - (SCARDBs):**
At the state level there is State Co-operative Agriculture and Rural Development Banks - (SCARDBs) up to 31st March, 2003 the number of SCARDBs were 20.

2) **Primary Co-operative Agriculture and Rural Development Banks - (PCARDBs):**
At the district level there are Primary Co-operative Agriculture and Rural Development Banks - (PCARDBs). On 31st March 2003 the number of PCARDBs was 768. In some states the structure of Long-term co-operative credit institutions is of unitary while in some other states it is of two tier system. States in which long-term co-operative credit institutions are not in operation, State Co-operative Banks render banking services through the branches of Regional Rural Banks and urban and semi-urban branches of commercial banks in those states.

However, in the state of Andhra Pradesh, the structure of co-operatives is of unitary nature and within that long-term and short-term co-operative structure is integrated. Thus, there is network of co-operative banks speeded all over India and the role of this banking plays a significant role in financing agriculture. There is a control of the State Government, the Reserve Bank of India and the National Bank for Agriculture and Rural Development (NABARD) over these co-operative banks. Due to this control and increasing number of co-operative banks, these banks have to face so many challenges. Co-operative banks are under the control of the State Government in case of registration, membership, election, financial assistance, power of disbursement of loans. Banking activities, recovery of loans and auditing and banking transactions are controlled and supervised by the NABARD and the Reserve Bank of India. The urban co-operative banks function under the control of the Reserve Bank of India whereas the rural co-operative credit institutions function under the control of the NABARD.

## 1.4 Role of Co-operative Banking in Economic Development:

In the agro-based developing economy like India, role of co-operative banking is as follows:

1) **A Ray of the Hope:**
When the socially weak and helpless persons come together on the principle of equality and try to raise their financial level by helping each other, they set up a co-operative institution. In case of a poor country like India more than 65 percent people live on agriculture and they are stricken by poverty, ignorance and exploitation. Therefore, for eradication of their poverty and unemployment and miserable life co-operative movement is a ray of hope.

2) **Encouragement to Savings:**
Co-operative banks create habits of economy and savings among their members. Similarly, they impart education of banking transactions. Co-operative banks meet

the economic needs of the general public at the local level. The important function of co-operative banks is to raise the level of savings of the general public.

**3) Supply of CREDIT:**

Near about 74% population lives in villages and agriculture is the main occupation of this population. Small, medium and big farmers require short term, medium term and long term loans. Co-operative banks and credit societies play a vital role in making the availability of the supply of credits to these people.

**4) Improvement in the Standard of LIVING:**

As co-operative banks provide loans to agriculture, the loans contribute to increase production, productivity of agriculture and incomes of the class of farmers. Due to rise in income of the common farmers, their standard of living improves.

**5) Freedom from the Clutches of Money Lenders:**

Before existence of co-operative banks, farmers were provided credits by the class of money lenders, merchants and landlords. In the year 1951, nearly 93 percent of loans were supplied by the private sources. Today also this proportion is 42 percent. Money lenders and landlords make cruel exploitation of farmers while supplying loans to them. If there is spreading of area of operations of co-operative banks far and wide, it will help the poor farmers to get rid of clutches of money lenders.

**6) Inducement to Rural Development:**

Co-operative banks under take different activities for rural development in addition to their credit supply to farmers. Co-operative banks supply loans at the concessional rate of interest and in easy installments to economically and socially weak sections of population to whom commercial banks do not give financial assistance. This leads to inducement to productive activities. So, productive investment is induced and the rural development gets direction in a proper way with the development of farmers.

**7) National Benefits:**

Co-operative banks perform banking business in the rural area. So, people in villages form habit of savings and investments. New progressive approach is created in the rural area. This ultimately gives benefit to people and the whole nation.

**8) Instrument of Economic Change:**

Co-operative banks in underdeveloped economy not only do the function of the acceptance of deposits and supply of credit. They also impart education of conducting democratic institutions through their working. The co-operative banks play the role of the economic and social change.

**9) Organisation of Weak People:**

Co-operative society is the organisation of weak and vulnerable group of people who come together on the basis of equality to help each other for enhancing their economic welfare. In a poor country like India with 60% of its people living on agriculture, suffering from illiteracy, exploitation poverty and unemployment, co-operative movement is the only hope for them.

## 1.5 Performance and Challenges before Co-operative Banking in India:

Co-operative banks play a vital role as it established to provide financial service to rural masses in India. They have established with the motive of financial inclusion and upliftment of rural economy. They play significant role in the social and economic development of India.

### 1.5.1 Performance of Co-operative Banks:

To evaluate the performance of Co-operative banks some variables have been studies like numbers of braches, total deposit, productivity per staff and branch, percentage of overdue to demand, NPA and profitability etc.

**Table No 1: Progress of number of branches of Co-operative banks in India**

| Year | SCB | % Change | DCCBs | % Change | PACS | % Change |
|---|---|---|---|---|---|---|
| 2009-10 | 1015 | | 13238 | | 89523 | |
| 2010-11 | 1028 | 1.28% | 13327 | 0.67% | 90279 | 0.84% |
| 2011-12 | 1047 | 1.85% | 13495 | 1.26% | 92432 | 2.38% |
| 2012-13 | 1081 | 3.25% | 13655 | 1.19% | 90958 | -1.59% |
| 2013-14 | 1096 | 1.39% | 13811 | 1.14% | 93042 | 2.29% |
| 2014-15 | 1131 | 3.19% | 14060 | 1.80% | 92789 | -0.27% |
| 2015-16 | 1168 | 3.27% | 14241 | 1.29% | 93367 | 0.62% |
| 2016-17 | 1197 | 2.48% | 14252 | 0.08% | 95595 | 2.39% |
| Average | 1095.37 | | 13757.59 | | 92248 | |
| CV | 6.02% | | 2.89% | | 1.97% | |
| CAGR | 2% | | 1% | | 1% | |

***Source:*** *Complied data from various annual reports of SCB, DCCB and PACS (2009-10-2016-17) which is available at website http://nafscob.org/*

Above table no 1 refers the progress of SCB, DCCB and PACS in number of branches. The number of branches SCB has increased from 1015 in 2010-11 to 1197 in 2016-17. In terms of number of branches of DCCB increased from 13238 to 14252 with CAGR 1% during study period. Number of branches of PACS increased from 89523 to 95595 with CAGR 1% during study period. The CAGR is more found of SCB with 2 % which is than DCCB and PACS. The value of Coefficient of variance is more found with 6.02 % than DCCB and PACS which indicates fewer consistent or more variable during study period. **Deposit Mobilization:** The deposits are the greatest liability of the bank. The deposit is the life blood in the banking institution. It determines the working and viability of the bank. The performance of deposit of co-operative is shown in table no 2

**Table No 2: Total Deposits of Co-operative banks in Maharashtra (Amt. in Crore)**

| Year | SCB | Growth | DCCBs | Growth | PACS | Growth |
|---|---|---|---|---|---|---|
| 2009-10 | 84838 | | 146364 | | 35680 | |
| 2010-11 | 81664 | -4% | 161309 | 10% | 37282 | 4% |
| 2011-12 | 86653 | 6% | 176711 | 10% | 54763 | 47% |
| 2012-13 | 89905 | 4% | 195726 | 11% | 37561 | -31% |
| 2013-14 | 101970 | 13% | 215662 | 10% | 81895 | 118% |
| 2014-15 | 100791 | -1% | 251116 | 16% | 84616 | 3% |
| 2015-16 | 104922 | 4% | 282609 | 13% | 101065 | 19% |
| 2016-17 | 121689 | 16% | 311858 | 10% | 115884 | 15% |
| Average | 96554 | | 217669.37 | | 68593.25 | |
| CV | 12.9% | | 25.4% | | 42.9% | |
| CAGR | 5% | | 11% | | 18% | |

***Source:*** *Same as table no 1*

It is reveals from the table total deposit of SCBs has increased from 84838 Crore to 121689 Crore from 2009-10- to 2016-17. Total deposit of SCB, DCCB and PACS have shown upward trend with CAGR 5%, 11% and 18 % respectively. The average total deposit was more found with 217669.37 Crore of DCCBs compared to others. The value of Coefficient of variance is more found with 42.9% of PACS which indicates less consistent. The value of Coefficient of variance is less found with 12.9% of SCBs which indicates more consistent.

**Table 3: Productivity per staff and per branch of Co-operative banks in India**

| Year | Productivity per staff | | | Productivity per Branch | | |
|---|---|---|---|---|---|---|
| | SCB | DCCBs | PACS | SCB | DCCBs | PACS |
| 2009-10 | 971.93 | 862.82 | 53.90 | 13196.26 | 5737.47 | 129.76 |
| 2010-11 | 999.11 | 336.39 | 40.20 | 13082.75 | 2219.41 | 129.36 |
| 2011-12 | 1221.29 | 461.88 | 75.82 | 15500.00 | 2943.31 | 171.18 |
| 2012-13 | 1464.82 | 465.69 | 61.26 | 16297.35 | 2919.71 | 141.53 |
| 2013-14 | 1486.71 | 482.89 | 119.72 | 17950.39 | 2954.38 | 227.80 |
| 2014-15 | 1582.69 | 240.57 | 141.00 | 17728.65 | 1426.11 | 249.86 |
| 2015-16 | 1748.17 | 626.05 | 147.18 | 19307.70 | 3681.79 | 277.99 |
| 2016-17 | 1905.86 | 630.51 | 165.94 | 20418.38 | 3678.95 | 299.54 |
| CAGR | 10% | -4% | 17% | 105% | -6% | 13% |

***Source:*** *Same as table no 1*

It is observed from above table 3, productivity per employee of SCB was found more which increased to 1905.86 from 2009-10 to 2016-17 than productivity per employee of DCCB and PACS. Productivity per branch of SCB was found more with

13196.26 increased to 20418.38 from 2009-10 to 2016-17 than productivity per branch of DCCB and PACS. The compound annual growth rate of Productivity per Staff and productivity per branch was more found with 17 % and 13 % of PACS respectively than SCB and DCCBs.

**Table No 4: Percentage of Overdue to Demand of Co-operative banks in India**

| Year | SCB | DCCBs | PACS |
|---|---|---|---|
| 2009-10 | 8.2 | 26.64 | 41.36 |
| 2010-11 | 7.69 | 27.37 | 24.99 |
| 2011-12 | 3.86 | 21.88 | 24.79 |
| 2012-13 | 5.18 | 20.37 | 26.67 |
| 2013-14 | 4.35 | 21.78 | 19.01 |
| 2014-15 | 4.48 | 20.92 | 22.42 |
| 2015-16 | 4.42 | 20.08 | 17.60 |
| 2016-17 | 3.56 | 23.33 | 26.58 |

Overdue problem is not good for the any bank. If the outstanding loan increases, it becomes overdue. Percentage of Overdue to Demand ratio shows that part of outstanding receivable amount that is in late payment. In above table no 4 noticed that ratio of percentage of overdue to demand of SCBs has decline from 8.2 percent to 3.56 percent during study period. It indicates the good recovery of SCBs in recent years In case of DCCBs, percentage of overdue to demand was also showed a declined trend from 26.36 percent to 20.08 percent from 2009-10 to 2015-16 but after that it rose to 23.33 percent in 2016-17. In terms of PACS, percentage of overdue to demand ratio is more than SCBs and DCCBs. Percentage of overdue to demand ratio was highest 41.36 percent in 2009-10 which reduced to down 24.99 percent in 2010-11, after that percentage of overdue to demand ratio has fluctuated and stood at 26.58 percent in 2016-17.

**Table No 5: Gross NPA of SCB and DCCB in India (%)**

| Year | SCBs | DCCBs |
|---|---|---|
| 2009-10 | 11.06 | 16.70 |
| 2010-11 | 9.12 | 16.98 |
| 2011-12 | 7.84 | 11.59 |
| 2012-13 | 9.12 | 10.12 |
| 2013-14 | 3.30 | 11.37 |
| 2014-15 | 4.62 | 11.13 |
| 2015-16 | 4.35 | 9.83 |
| 2016-17 | 2.85 | 9.39 |

***Source:*** *Same as table no 1*

Non-performing asset during the eight years is shown in table no 5, percentage of NPA of SCB which was high with 11.06 %, 9.12 %, 7.84 % and 9.12 % in the year 2009-10, 201011, 2011-12 and 2012-13. But after that it continuously reduced to 2.85 % in 2016-17, In terms of NPA of DCCBs has also shown little improvement which was reduced from 16.70 percent in 2009-10 to 9.39 percent in the year 2016-17.

Profitability is the most important thing for the existence of any business entity. It shows the overall strength and weakness of the bank. As considering the profits and loss of co-operative banks in India have been shown in table no 6.

**Table No 6: Profit and Loss of Co-operative banks in India (Amt. in lakhs)**

| Year | SCB | % Change | DCCBs | % Change | PACS | % Change |
|---|---|---|---|---|---|---|
| 2009-10 | -16567 | | 265476 | | -113895.51 | |
| 2010-11 | -13139 | -21% | 3752 | -99% | -19157.77 | -83% |
| 2011-12 | -6280 | -52% | 116080 | 2994% | -202183.56 | 955% |
| 2012-13 | 53682 | -955% | 102904 | -11% | -213035.65 | 5% |
| 2013-14 | 61417 | 14% | 90192 | -12% | --193423.26 | -9% |
| 2014-15 | 84067 | 37% | 90555 | 0% | -154896.91 | -20% |
| 2015-16 | 109655 | 30% | 143761 | 59% | -240047.96 | 55% |
| 2016-17 | 112907 | 3% | 83723 | -42% | -326313.23 | 36% |
| Average | 48217.8 | | 112055.37 | | -410826.75 | |
| CV | 105% | | 62% | | -149% | |

***Source:*** *Same as table no 1*

It is observed from the above table that initially SCBs were in loss with 16567 lakhs in 2009-10 and 6280 lakhs in 2011-12. But after 2012-13 SCB were getting continuously profit with 53682 lakhs in 2012-13 which increased to 112907 lakhs in 2016-17.

In case of DCCBs, profit has fluctuated during study period. The value of coefficient of variance of profit and loss profit was 105%, 62% and -149% of SCB, DCCB and PACS respectively. The value of coefficient of variance of profit and loss profit of PACS was -149% due to continuously they were in losses. The value of coefficient of variance of profit and loss profit of DCCB was 62 % which indicates less consistency of the data as compared to SCB and PACS.

## Graphical presentation of some variables of Co-operative Banks

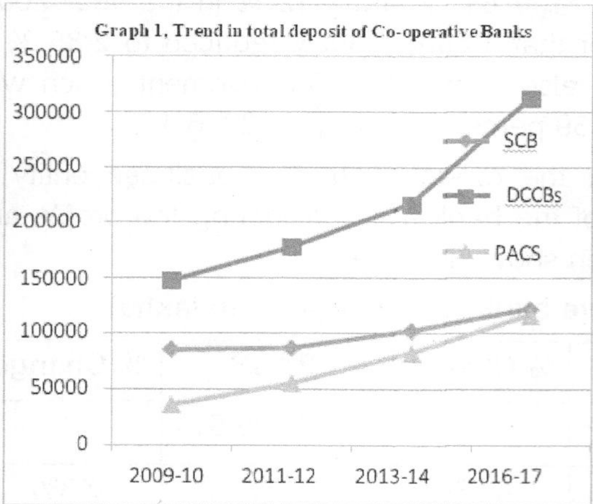


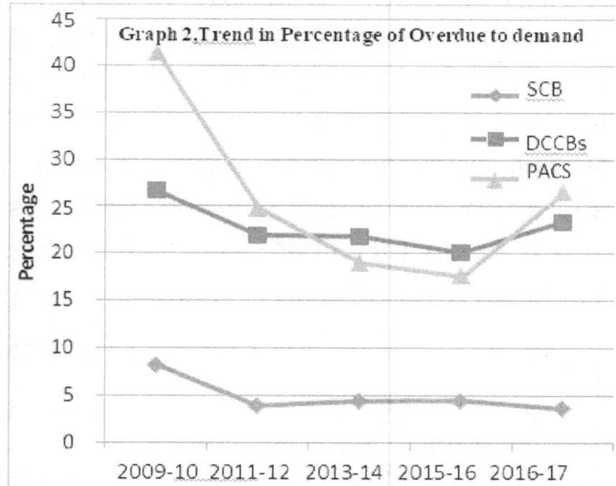


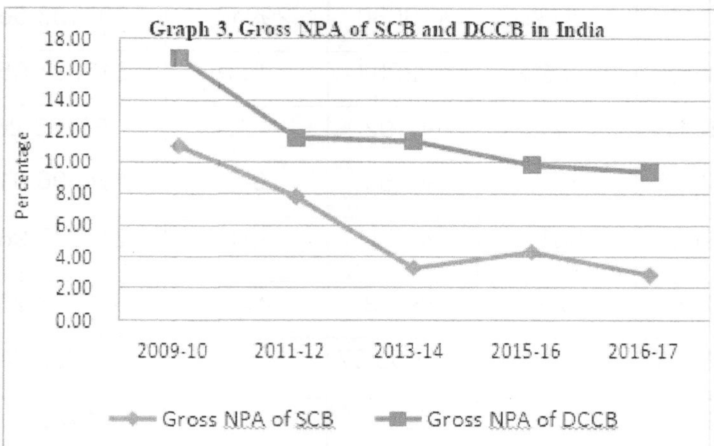


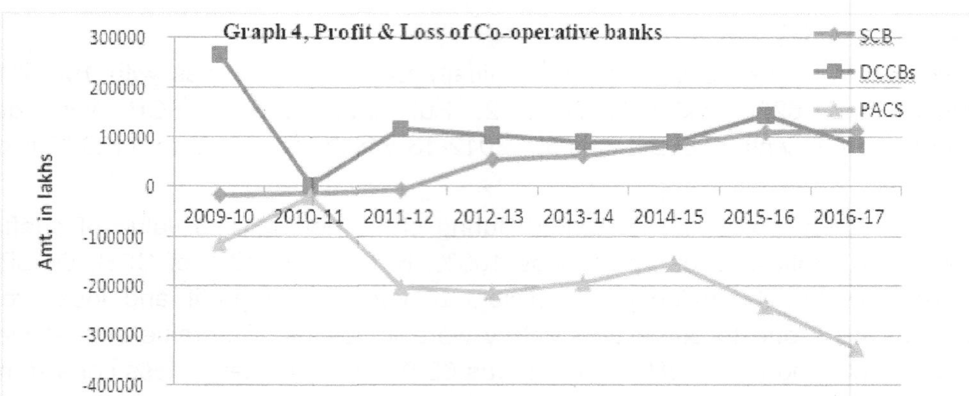

### 1.5.2 Challenges before Co-operative Banks:

There are some important snags and deficiencies in the working of co-operative credit societies and they have failed to acquire the dynamism needed to discharge their responsibilities. The All India Rural Credit Survey committee and other Committees have brought out the following deficiencies in the co-operative credit systems.

1) **Lack-of Spontaneity:**
   The movement was not voluntary and the people did not come forward to form societies to satisfy their economic needs. The villagers generally thought that the societies were government-lending institutions.
2) **Lack of Funds:**
   The basic feature of co-operative banking system must be a large reliance on resources mobilized locally and a lesser and lesser dependence on higher credit institutions. However, not only PACS but also the higher credit institutions, viz., DCCBs and SCBs could not attract as much deposits from the general public as was anticipated.
3) **Loans for Productive Purpose only:**
   Co-operatives give loans only for agricultural operations. However, farmers need credit for consumption purpose also. Hence, they either depend on money lenders or they divert the production loans to meet unproductive purposes which in turn lead to overdue problem.
4) **Production Credit only:**
   The Co-operatives have failed to appreciate the link between credit and processing and marketing. What is really needed is a co-operative society which would integrate various aspects of agricultural operations in order to meet all the needs of the farmers.
5) **Non-viable Units:**
   A viable unit is one which renders the more important services adequately to as many members as possible within a reasonable time. According to NAFSCOB estimates, 62 percent of the PACS in the country are viable, 30 percent are potentially viable and eight percent are either dormant, defunct or under liquidation during 2007-08.
6) **Uneven Growth:**
   The development of co-operative movement indicated that the progress in different parts of the country has been uneven.
7) **Mounting over Dues:**
   The financial soundness of co-operative credit structure depends on the prompt recovery of loans. The problem of over dues affects not only the interests of the defaulters themselves, but also the other regularly repaying members, creditors, and the very co-operative movement itself.

**8) Defective Management and Leadership:**

The failure or non-viability of co-operative credit societies is also due to defective management and leadership. The officials do not have proper training and hence they could not compete with money lenders or private lending agencies.

**9) Interference of the Government:**

The Government attempts to convert co-operatives into a government department with all its rigidities and short-sightedness associated with a government department. Government also did not take adequate interest in improving the financial strength of the societies. It also resorts to ban or postponement of recovery of loans which hampers the functioning of societies.

**10) Delayed Credit:**

A common complaint is that farmers do not get loans in time. So credit delayed is credit denied. Delayed credit tempts the borrower to divert it to other unproductive purposes.

## Review Questions

**Q.1 Answers in 100 Words:**

1) Explain the Concept of Cooperation.
2) Discuss the Meaning of Cooperative Banking.
3) Explain the Short-term Structure of Cooperative Banking.
4) Write the Long-term Structure of Cooperative Banking.
5) State the Contribution of Service Sector in Indian Economy.

**Q.2 Answers in 200 Words:**

1) Explain the Evolution of Cooperative Banking in India.
2) Discuss the Structure of Cooperative Banking in India.
3) Explain the Role of Cooperative Banks in Rural Development.
4) Explain the Challenges of Cooperative Banking in India.

**Q.3 Answers in 300 Words:**

1) What is Cooperation? Explain the Principles of Cooperation.
2) Explain the Meaning and Significance of Cooperative Banking in India.
3) Discuss in detail Performance of Cooperative Banking in India.

**Q.4 Write Short Note on Following:**

1) Concept of Cooperation.
2) Meaning of Cooperative Banking.
3) Structure of Cooperative Banking.
4) Challenges of Cooperative Banking.

★★★★★★★

**UNIT 2**

# Development Banks in India

**2.1 Concept of Development Banking**

**2.2 Features of Development Banking**

**2.3 Functions of Development Banks**

**2.4 Role of Development Banks in Economic Development**

**2.5 Challenges before Development Banking in India**

## Introduction:

The concept of development banking is a new concept which was used for the first time in the post Second World War period to refer to the institutional financial machinery built for fostering industrial growth in the country. After the Second World War, several newly liberated underdeveloped countries in Asia. Africa and Latin America became restless and wanted to solve their chronic problems of squalor and poverty. In India, the emergence of development banking is a post-independence phenomenon. An outstanding financial development of the post-independence period has been the rapid growth of development banks in the country. These banks are specialised financial institutions which perform the twin functions of providing medium and long-term finance to private entrepreneurs and of performing various promo-tional roles conducive to economic development. The concept of development banking is a new concept which was used for the first time in the post Second World War period to refer to the institutional financial machinery built for fostering industrial growth in the country. After the Second World War, several newly liberated underdeveloped countries in Asia. Africa and Latin America became restless and wanted to solve their chronic problems of squalor and poverty. For the rapid industrial growth of the country and to supply the basic ingredients of development like capital, knowledge and entrepreneurship they established special financial institutions. In India, the emergence of development banking is a post-independence phenomenon.

## 2.1 Concept of Development Banking:

Development banks were established mainly for the purpose of promotion and development the industrial sector in the country. Presently, large numbers of development banks are functioning with multidimensional activities. Development banks are also called as financial institutions or statutory financial institutions or statutory non-banking institutions. Development banks provide two important types of finance:

**a)** Direct Finance

**b)** Indirect Finance/Refinance

Presently the commercial banks are providing all kinds of financial services including development-banking services. And also nowadays development banks and specialisted financial institutions are providing all kinds of financial services including commercial banking services. Diversified and global financial services are unavoidable to the present day economics. Hence, we can classify the financial institutions only by the structure and set up and not by the services provided by them.

### 2.1.1 Evolution:

The concept of development banking originated during the post Second World War period. Many countries of Europe were in the stage of industrial development and special financial institutions known as development banks were setup to foster industrial growth. In the US, development finance institutions came into existence for special purposes such as economic rehabilitation and filling gaps in the traditional financing pattern. Not only developed countries, but several underdeveloped countries in Asia, Africa and Latin America established special financial institutions to hasten the pace of industrialisation and growth. The International Bank for Reconstruction and Development (IBRD) known as the World Bank and the International Monetary Fund (IMF) are examples of development banks at the international level. The major objective of the World Bank is to promote world development and perform the task of transfer of enormous financial and technical resources from the developed to developing nations. The IMF performs a special function of providing financial assistance to private sector projects in developing countries.

### 2.1.2 Meaning:

A development bank is a 'bank' established for the purpose of 'financing development'. A traditional definition of a development bank is one which is a national or regional financial institution designed to provide medium-and long-term capital for productive investment, often accompanied by technical assistance, in less-developed areas. Development banks fill a gap left by undeveloped capital markets and the reluctance of commercial banks to offer long-term financing. The terms 'development bank' and 'development finance institution' are synonymous with each other although the term 'development bank' represents a simpler language. In some context, however, the term 'development finance institution' is appropriate to use because the term 'bank' connotes, among others, a deposit-taking activity, which in some countries DFIs are not allowed to undertake. But in the context of 'financing development', both terms, however, are used interchangeably.

## 2.1.3 Definitions:

Following are the definitions of development banks:

1) **Prof. William Diamond:**

   *"Development bank is one which encourages new enterprises, provides them capital and thus helps in industrial development."*

2) **Dr. K.V. Prabhakar:**

   *"Development bank is a multipurpose institution, which shares the organizational risk, changes its policy as per the industrial environment and encourages new industrial projects."*

3) **Shri B.K. Madan:**

   *"Development bank is an institution which not only supplies capital to industries but also provides them technical and managerial advice and helps in sale and management."*

4) **In General sense:**

   *"Development banks are those financial institutions whose prime goal (motive) is to finance the primary (basic) needs of the society. Such funding results in the growth and development of social and economic sectors of the nation. However, needs of the society vary from region to region due to differences seen in its communal structure, economy and other aspects."*

5) **As per Banking Subject (mainly in Indian context):**

   *"Development banks are financial institutions established to lend (loan) finance (money) on subsidized interest rate. Such lending is sanctioned to promote and develop important sectors like agriculture, industry, import-export, housing and allied activities."*

## 2.1.3 Development Banks in India:

Development banking was started after the World War II. It provided finance to reconstruct the buildings and industries which were destroyed in the war. In India, development banking was started immediately after independence. The arrangement of development banks in India is depicted below.

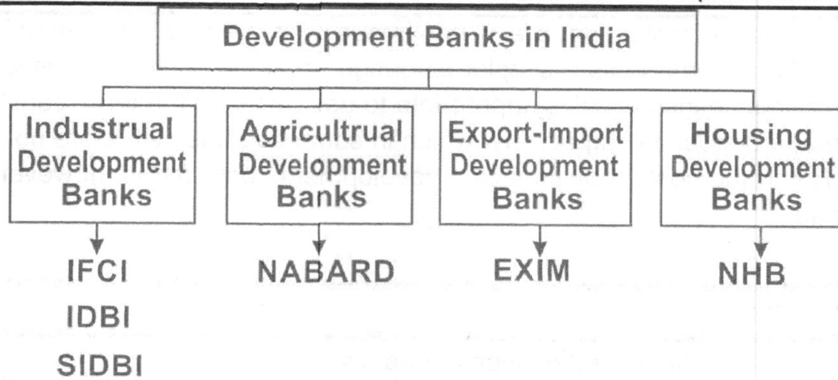


Development banks in India are classified into following four groups:

1) **Industrial Development Banks:**
   It includes, for example, Industrial Finance Corporation of India (IFCI), Industrial Development Bank of India (IDBI), and Small Industries Development Bank of India (SIDBI).
2) **Agricultural Development Banks:**
   It includes, for example, National Bank for Agriculture & Rural Development (NABARD).
3) **Export-Import Development Banks:**
   It includes, for example, Export-Import Bank of India (EXIM Bank).
4) **Housing Development Banks:**
   It includes, for example, National Housing Bank (NHB).

Industrial Finance Corporation of India (IFCI) is the first development bank in India. It started in 1948 to provide finance to medium and large-scale industries in India.

## 2.2 Features of Development Banking:

Following are the features of development banking:

1) **It is a Financial Institution:**
   It distributes its share capital, debentures to people and collects funds, which are used for giving loans. It is an institution functioning in accordance with the banking rules.
2) **Multipurpose Financial Institute:**
   These banks help in starting new projects, in raising capital, guide in the purchase of machines, vehicles etc., provide advice for running an enterprise, guide in the purchase of raw material and sale of finished products and help in other respects also.
3) **Medium & Long-term Loans to Business Firms:**
   These banks provide medium and long term loan assistance to economically viable business units.

**4) Don't accept Deposits:**

These banks don't accept deposits from the people like commercial banks. General public cannot open current, savings or recurring accounts with these banks.

**5) Expert Institution:**

These banks appoint experts from various fields like industry, commerce, agriculture and take their help. These banks function in consultation with these experts. Borrowers therefore, can avail their advice at concessional rate fee.

**6) Developmental Finance:**

These banks help in the process of economic development by making finance available to the productive units. These units, which have the potential of survival, which can withstand competition, are assisted by the development banks.

**7) Encouragement to the Investment and Entrepreneurship:**

These banks not only assist existing units but also motivate setting up of new units, and help them in their further development.

**8) More stress on Implementation:**

These banks do not merely provide finance, but guide industrial units in deciding location of plant, in the purchase and installation of machinery, in the production and management of the unit and also in the sale of final produce. Development banks assist industrial & other units so that they will succeed and others will draw lessons from them.

**9) Inspiration to New and Small Units:**

Experts of these development banks motivate new and small business units for their development.

**10) Social and Economic Objectives:**

These banks work for the achievement of those objectives which will promote overall development of the country.

**11) Encouragement to Saving and Investment:**

As these banks promote the development of new and existing business units, they indirectly help in improving savings and investment levels in the economy.

**12) Objective of Social well-being:**

The development banks function for the social well-being by assisting in the development of both public and private business units from industry, commerce and trade, agriculture, services. They provide advice and guidance for the success of these business units. Thus, these banks work for the improvement of social well-being.

## 2.3 Functions of Development Banking:

The nine important functions of development banks in India are as follows:

**1) Small Scale Industries (SSI):**

Development banks play an important role in the promotion and development of the small-scale sector. Government of India (GOI) started Small industries Development Bank of India (SIDBI) to provide medium and long-term loans to Small Scale Industries (SSI) units. SIDBI provides direct project finance and equipment finance to SSI units. It also refinances banks and financial institutions that provide seed capital, equipment finance, etc., to SSI units.

**2) Development of Housing Sector:**

Development banks provide finance for the development of the housing sector. GOI started the National Housing Bank (NHB) in 1988. NHB promotes the housing sector in the following ways:

**a)** It promotes and develops housing and financial institutions.

**b)** It refinances banks and financial institutions that provide credit to the housing sector.

**3) Large Scale Industries (LSI):**

Development banks promote and develop large-scale industries (LSI). Development financial institutions like IDBI, IFCI, etc., provide medium and long-term finance to the corporate sector. They provide merchant banking services, such as preparing project reports, doing feasibility studies, advising on location of a project, and so on.

**4) Agriculture and Rural Development:**

Development banks like National Bank for Agriculture & Rural Development (NABARD) helps in the development of agriculture. NABARD started in 1982 to provide refinance to banks, which provide credit to the agriculture sector and also for rural development activities. It coordinates the working of all financial institutions that provide credit to agriculture and rural development. It also provides training to agricultural banks and helps to conduct agricultural research.

**5) Enhance the Foreign Trade of India:**

Development banks help to promote foreign trade. Government of India started Export-Import Bank of India (EXIM Bank) in 1982 to provide medium and long-term loans to exporters and importers from India. It provides Overseas Buyers Credit to buy Indian capital goods. It also encourages abroad banks to provide finance to the buyers in their country to buy capital goods from India.

**6) Review of Sick Industrial Units:**

Development banks help to revive (cure) sick-units. Govemment of India (GOI) started Industrial investment Bank of India (IIBI) to help sick units. IIBI is the main credit and reconstruction institution for revival of sick units. It facilitates modernization, restructuring and diversification of sick-units by providing credit and other services.

**7) Entrepreneurship Development:**

Many development banks facilitate entrepreneurship development. NABARD, State Industrial Development Banks and State Finance Corporations provide training to entrepreneurs in developing leadership and business management skills. They conduct seminars and workshops for the benefit of entrepreneurs.

**8) Regional Development:**

Development banks facilitate rural and regional development. They provide finance for starting companies in backward areas. They also help the companies in project management in such less-developed areas.

**9) Contribution to Capital Markets:**

Development banks contribute the growth of capital markets. They invest in equity shares and debentures of various companies listed in India. They also invest in mutual funds and facilitate the growth of capital markets in India.

## 2.4 Role of Development Banks in Economic Development:

Development banks have been started with the motive of increasing the pace of industrialization. The traditional financial institutions could not take up this challenge because of their limitations. To help all round industrialization development banks were made multipurpose institutions. Besides financing, they were assigned promotional work also. Their role in the economic development is as follows:

**1) To fill the Financial Gap:**

Development banks do not provide medium-term and long-term loans only but they help industrial enterprises in many other ways too. These banks subscribe to the bonds and debentures of the companies, underwrite their shares and debentures and, guarantee the loans rose from foreign and domestic sources. They also help undertakings to acquire machinery from within and outside the country.

**2) To undertake Entrepreneurial Role:**

Developing countries lack entrepreneurs who can take up the job of setting up new projects. It may be due to a lack of expertise and managerial ability. Development banks were assigned the job of entrepreneurial gap filling. They undertake the task of discovering investment projects, promotion of industrial enterprises, provide technical and managerial assistance, undertaking economic and technical research, conducting surveys, feasibility studies, etc. The promotional role of the development bank is very significant for increasing the pace of industrialization. It may also not be possible to meet all the requirements of concern by one institution, so more than one institution may join hands. Not only in large projects but also in medium-sized projects it may be desirable for a concern to have, for instance, the requirements of a foreign loan in a particular currency, met by one institution and under the writing of securities met by another.

**3) To Provide Refinance Facility:**

Development banks also extend the refinance facility to the lending institutions. In this scheme, there is no direct lending to the enterprise. The lending institutions are provided funds by development banks against loans extended' to industrial concerns. In this way, the institutions which provide funds to units are refinanced by development banks. In India, the Industrial Development Bank of India (IDBI) provides reliance against term loans granted to industrial concerns by state financial corporations.

**4) To support for Commercial Banking Business:**

Development banks normally provide medium and long-term funds to industrial enterprises. The working capital needs of the units are met by commercial banks. In developing countries, commercial banks have not been able to take up this job properly. Their traditional approach in dealing with lending proposals and assistance on securities has not helped the industry. Development banks extend financial assistance for meeting working capital needs to their loan if they fail to arrange such funds from other sources. So far as taking up other functions of banks such as accepting of deposits, opening letters of credit, discounting of bills, etc. there is no uniform practice in development banks.

**5) To provide the facility of Joint Finance:**

Another feature of the development bank's operations is to take up joint financing along with other financial institutions. There may be constraints of financial resources and legal problems (prescribing maximum limits of lending) which may force banks to associate with other institutions for taking up the financing of some projects jointly.

**6) To support for Credit Guarantee:**

The small scale sector is not getting proper financial facilities due to the clement of risk since these units do not have sufficient securities to offer for loans, lending institutions are hesitant to extend the loans. To overcome this difficulty many countries including India and Japan have devised the credit guarantee scheme and credit insurance scheme.

**7) To underwrite Securities:**

Development banks acquire securities of industrial units through either direct subscribing or underwriting or both. The securities may also be acquired through promotion work or by converting loans into equity shares or preference shares. So, as learn about development banks may build portfolios of industrial stocks and bonds. These banks do not hold these securities permanently. They try to disinvest in these securities in a systematic way which should not influence the market prices of these securities and also should not lose managerial control of the units. Development banks have become worldwide phenomena. Their functions depend upon the requirements of the economy and the state of development of the country.

They have become well-recognized segments of the financial market. They are playing an important role in the promotion of industries in developing and underdeveloped countries.

## 2.5 Challenges before Development Banking in India:

Developing countries like India still have a huge number of people who do not have access to banking services due to scattered and fragmented locations. But if we talk about those people who are availing banking services, their expectations are raising as the level of services are increasing due to the emergence of Information Technology and competition. Since, foreign banks are playing in Indian market, the number of services offered has increased and banks have laid emphasis on meeting the customer expectations. Now, the existing situation has created various challenges and opportunity for Indian Commercial Banks. In order to encounter the general scenario of banking industry, we need to understand the challenges and opportunities lying with banking industry of India.

**1) Rural Market:**

Banking in India is generally fairly mature in terms of supply, product range and reach, even though reach in rural India still remains a challenge for the private sector and foreign banks. In terms of quality of assets and capital adequacy, Indian banks are considered to have clean, strong and transparent balance sheets relative to other banks in comparable economies in its region. Consequently, we have seen some examples of inorganic growth strategy adopted by some nationalized and private sector banks to face upcoming challenges in banking industry of India.

**2) Growth of Banking:**

Zhao, Casu and Ferrari (2008) used a balanced panel data set covering the period of 1992- 2004 and employing a Data Envelopment Analysis (DEA)-based Malmquist Total Factor Productivity (TFP) index. The empirical study indicated that, after an initial adjustment phase, the Indian banking industry experienced sustained productivity growth, which was driven mainly by technological progress. Banks' ownership structure does not seem to matter as much as increased competition in TFP growth. Foreign banks appear to have acted as technological innovators when competition increased, which added to the competitive pressure in the banking market. Finally, our results also indicate an increase in risk-taking behaviour, along with the whole deregulation process.

**3) Human Resource Management:**

Gelade and Ivery (2003) examined relationships between human resource management (HRM), work climate, and organizational performance in the branch network of a retail bank. Significant correlations were found between work climate, human resource practices, and business performance. The results showed that the correlations between climate and performance cannot be explained by their common dependence on HRM factors, and that the data are consistent with a mediation model in which the effects of HRM practices on business performance are partially mediated by work climate.

**4) Global Banking:**

It is practically and fundamentally impossible for any nation to exclude itself from world economy. Therefore, for sustainable development, one has to adopt integration process in the form of liberalization and globalization as India spread the red carpet for foreign firms in 1991. The impact of globalization becomes challenges for the domestic enterprises as they are bound to compete with global players. If we look at the Indian Banking Industry, then we find that there are 36 foreign banks operating in India, which becomes a major challenge for Nationalized and private sector banks. These foreign banks are large in size, technically advanced and having presence in global market, which gives more and better options and services to Indian traders.

**5) Financial Inclusion:**

Financial inclusion has become a necessity in today's business environment. Whatever is produced by business houses, that has to be under the check from various perspectives like environmental concerns, corporate governance, social and ethical issues. Apart from it, to bridge the gap between rich and poor, the poor people of the country should be given proper attention to improve their economic condition. Dev (2006) stated that financial inclusion is significant from the point of view of living conditions of poor people, farmers, rural non-farm enterprises and other vulnerable groups. Apart from formal banking institutions, which should look at inclusion both as a business opportunity and social responsibility, the author conclude that role of the self-help group movement and microfinance institutions is important to improve financial inclusion. The study suggested that this requires new regulatory procedures and de-politicisation of the financial system. Employees' Retention: The banking industry has transformed rapidly in the last ten years, shifting from transactional and customer service-oriented to an increasingly aggressive environment, where competition for revenue is on top priority. Long-time banking employees are becoming disenchanted with the industry and are often resistant to perform upto new expectations. The diminishing employee morale results in decreased revenue. Due to the intrinsically close ties between staff and clients, losing those employees completely can mean the loss of valuable customer relationships. Mitchell, Holtom, Lee and Graske (2001) asserted in their study that people often leave for reasons unrelated to their jobs. In many cases, unexpected events or shocks are the cause. Employees also often stay because of attachments and their sense of fit, both on the job and in their community.

**6) Customer Retention:**

Levesque and McDougall (1996) investigated the major determinants of customer satisfaction and future intentions in the retail bank sector. They identified the determinants which include service quality dimensions (e.g. getting it right the first time), service features (e.g. competitive interest rates), service problems, service recovery and products used. It was found, in particular, that service problems and the bank's service recovery ability have a major impact on customer satisfaction and intentions to switch.

**7) Environmental Concerns:**

It is quite clear from the recently formed Copenhagen Climate Council (CCC) that there is a severe need for environmental awareness among all the countries of the world. CCC published Thought Leadership Series on Climate Change which is a collection of inspirational concise and clearly argued pieces from some of the world's most renowned thinkers and business leaders on climate change.

**8) Social and Ethical Aspects:**

There are some banks, which proactively undertake the responsibility to bear the social and ethical aspects of banking. This is a challenge for commercial banks to consider these aspects in their working. Apart from profit maximization, commercial banks are supposed to support those organizations, which have some social concerns.

*******

## Review Questions

**Q.1 Answers in 100 Words:**

1) Explain the Evolution of Development Banking.
2) Discuss about the Development Banks in India.
3) Explain the Meaning and Definition of Development Banking.

**Q.2 Answers in 200 Words:**

1) Explain the Features of Development Banking.
2) Discuss the Functions of Development Banks.

**Q.3 Answers in 300 Words:**

1) What is Development Banking? Explain the Features of Development Banking.
2) Explain the Role of Development Banks in Economic Development.
3) State the Challenges before Development Banking in India.

**Q.4 Write Short Note on Following:**

1) Meaning of Development Banking.
2) Evolution of Development Banking.
3) Features of Development Banking.
4) Functions of Development Banks.

★★★★★★★

UNIT 3

# Banking Sector Reforms

- 3.1 Banking Sector Reforms in India
- 3.2 Narsimhan Committee – I
- 3.3 Narsimhan Committee – II
- 3.4 Banking Reforms Measures
- 3.5 Framework of Basel Committees on Banking Supervision

## Introduction:

Banking sector reforms have redefined the entire Indian banking landscape. However, banks are now facing a number of challenges such as technological change, stringent prudential norms, increasing competition, worrying level of nonperforming assets (NPA's), rising customer expectations, increasing pressure on profitability, rising operating expenditure and shrinking levels of spreads. Since nationalisation of banks in 1969, the banking sector had been dominated by the public sector. There was financial repression, role of technology was limited, no risk management etc. This resulted in low profitability and poor asset quality. The country was caught in deep economic crises. The Government decided to introduce comprehensive economic reforms. Banking sector reforms were part of this package. In august 1991, the Government appointed a committee on financial system under the chairmanship of M. Narasimhan.

## 3.1 Banking Sector Reforms in India:

The banking sector is the heart of all the economic activity of a country and a small change in its regulation affects the entire economy. The example we all have seen is demonetization and how it influenced every one of us. In this article, we are going to discuss the entire major Banking sector Reforms took place in India.

The Banking Sector is an important part of the economy. It monitors and regulates the smooth functioning of the Indian economy. The banking sector reforms acts are to promote the efficiency and productivity of the banking system in India. They aim to increase growth and development. They also maintain stability and adequacy in the financial market.

1) **Before Independence:**

Modern banking in India started way back to 1786, with the establishment of the General Bank of India. In 1806, the East India Company established the first Presidency Bank in Kolkata.

Two more banks were established in 1840 and 1843 named Bank of Bombay and Bank of Madras. Reserve Bank of India (RBI) came into formation on April 1, 1935, with the enactment 50 of the Reserve Bank of India Act, 1934.

The objective of establishing the Reserve Bank, as stated in the preamble to the RBI Act, was to "regulate the issue of banknotes and the keeping of reserves with a view of securing monetary stability in India".

2) **Post Independence:**

Even after independence, the banks were mainly urban-oriented and were beyond the reach of the rural population. A large section of the rural population still had to look upon the moneylenders as their resort for credit.

India's commercial banking system in 1991 had many of the problems typical of unreformed banking systems in many developing countries. There was extensive financial repression, reflected in detailed controls on interest rates, and large preemption of bank resources to finance the government deficit through the imposition of high statutory liquidity ratio (SLR), which prescribed investment in government securities at low interest rates. The system was also dominated by public sector banks, which accounted for 90 percent of total banking sector assets, reflecting the impact of two rounds of nationalization of private sector banks above a certain size, first in 1969 and again in 1983. These banks were nationalized because of the perception that it was necessary to impose social control over banking to give it a developmental thrust, with a special emphasis on extending banking in rural areas. The system suffered from inadequate prudential regulations, and nontransparent accounting practices. Supervision by the Reserve Bank of India (RBI) was also weak.

The strategy for banking reforms was broadly similar to that followed in other countries, but with some important differences. It was similar to the extent that it focused on imposing prudential norms and improving regulatory supervision to meet Basel I standards (standards that were formulated by the committee of the Bank of International Settlement, or BIS, based in Basel, Switzerland), and it aimed at increasing competition to promote greater efficiency. However, there were two important differences compared with reforms in other countries. First, the reforms in banking were much more gradualist than in most countries, a course of action that was in line with the general strategy of reforms in India, made possible by the fact that the reforms were not introduced in the midst of a banking sector crisis, which might have entailed greater urgency. Second, unlike the case in many other countries, there was never any intention to privatize public sector banks. It was clearly recognized that competition was desirable, and this implied that both private sector banks and foreign banks should be allowed to expand their market share if they could. However, the government also declared its intention to strengthen public sector banks and enable them to meet competition.

There was also a great deal of progress in introducing prudential norms for income recognition, asset classification, and capital adequacy in a phased manner. As a consequence of this gradualist process, income recognition norms and capital adequacy norms have been fully aligned with Basel I standards, while asset recognition norms, though still falling short of international best practice, are now close to existing international standards.

### 3.1.1 Meaning of Banking Sector Reforms in India:

It is the reform of the Indian banking sector under the objectives of solving the chronic nonprofit earning problems and strengthening of the overall health of the public sector banks to face international competitions. Banks are financial institutions which are licensed to take deposits from public and grant them loans. In that sense they differ from the traditional money lenders. The banking sector reforms in India are aimed at introduction of best international practices and technological changes for making the Indian banking sector competitive globally. The Indian banking system is more efficient and stable today. Consequently there has been a rapid increase in the number of banks in this country. The banking horizon is changing because of the increasing number of private banks and the foreign banks. Apparently there is a cut throat competition between the banks. Banks began to diversify their services as part of their corporate strategy to cater to various customer segments.

### 3.1.2 Goals of Banking Sector Reforms in India:

In post-independence India, a mixed economy and economic planning were adopted. Economic policies were implemented with the objective of construction of a socialist society. All this resulted in strengthening the public sector. Public responsibilities were given priority and outlook of profit was considered secondary. Instead of emphasizing qualitative improvement, quantitative development became more important. As a result, all sectors in Indian economy suffered from inefficiency, sickness, etc. Banking sector was not an exception to this. In 1990, India faced a grave economic crisis and Indian economy was at the threshold of economic bankruptcy. India had to mortgage 48 tons of gold to raise loans in order to come out of bankruptcy. After this development, Dr.

Manmohan Singh initiated the programme of economic reforms in 1991. Factors responsible for India's economic reform programme are thought to include pressures from IMF, World Bank, USA, developed capitalist European countries, fall of the Soviet Union along with the economic crisis. While responding to economic reforms, following objectives were finalised in order to bring improvement in banking and financial sectors:

1) To improve effectiveness and efficiency of banks and financial institutions particularly in respect of their profitability and responsibility.
2) To bring about improvements in banking business, financial systems, bank management, banking policies and procedure.
3) To create a proper and revitalising atmosphere so that suitable response is given to the new credit requirement as a result of economic reforms and transformation.
4) To supervise operations of Indian banking systems and financial institutions and to create a suitable mechanism for supervision.
5) To study the effect of policies of RBI and Government of India on business interests of banks and understand related recommendations.
6) To find out how policies of privatisation and liberalisation can be implemented in the banking sector.
7) To look for measures which can enhance competitive efficiency of the bank industry and to ensure growth technical skills, modernisation, mechanisation, etc. in banking operations.
8) To determine criteria of adequacy of capital of banks and property management with the purpose of maintaining safety and credibility of banking business.
9) To reconsider supervision method in banking industry in view of its growing nature, quantitative and structural development.
10) To examine the legal framework and structure of banking industry and to suggest suitable amendments.

Therefore, it was essential to attempt improvements in the reformist outlook on the banking industry. At the same time, a sharebroker named Harshad Mehta exploited the weak and non-transparent situation in banking and financial sector and took charge of the entire share-market. This share scam rocked the entire capital market. Many banks went bankrupt while many other banks suffered heavy losses resulting in down slide and disrepute of banking business. Against this background, Central Government appointed a high-level committee under the chairmanship of Narasihan to suggest improvements in banking business. Recommendations regarding reforms in the banking sector made by this committee are considered very important.

## 3.2 Narsimhan Committee - I:

In post-independence period, socialist and democratic planning advocated by Nehru was responsible for determination of direction and scope of development of Indian economy. In this initial period, socialist outlook was essential for the economy because of down slide of the economy over a long period of colonial rule, large scale economic imbalance, large population suffering from poverty, misery, ill health, etc. At that time, main objectives included quick resolution of socio-economic problems, leading Indian economy on the path of development, etc. A programme of reallocation of land and agricultural reform was taken up under land reform with the help of economic planning and socialist reconstructing. At the same time, efforts were made to establish basic industries development, internal structure expansion of banking and financial systems, increase in international trade, etc. In this period of rebirth of Indian economy, this policy adopted by India proved to be very useful. In the period of 40 years, this economic policy not only made the country self-sufficient in agricultural production but also caused remarkable growth in all sectors such as industry, trade, banking and financing system, service sector, transport and communication, international trade etc.

While Indian economy achieved quantitative growth, it faced new problems. In 1990, India faced economic crisis. Increasing bankruptcies, growing financial deficit, reversal of qualitative development, high rate of inflation, serious poverty and unemployment, corruption, bureaucracy, black-marketing, adverse balance of trade falling, international credibility, etc. created situation where fundamental changes in economic policy based on Government interference were absolutely required. In 1942 India had to make fundamental changes in economic policies in order to aim for qualitative development to adjust to changing international conditions and because of direct and indirect pressure from IMF, GATT, European Union, USA, etc. with the aid at new economic policy India adopted the policy of privatisation, liberalisation and globalisation.

### 3.2.1 Establishment:

Under the new economic policy Government of India appointed a high level committee under the chairmanship of ex-Government of RBI Shri M. Narasimhan on 14 August 1991 in the context of Indian banking and financial systems. This committee had 8 members. They included deputy Governor of RBI, Chairmen of SBI, ICICI, IDBI, Additional Secretary, Department of Finance, Government of India, Mr. Manu Shroff, Mr. Y. H. Melegan and Mr. M. D. Chowdhary were on the committee. In December 1997, a second committee under the chairmanship of M. Narasimhan was set up in order to make the bank reform programme more dynamic at the second stage of economic reforms. This committee submitted its report in 1998. Thus, reports one and two regarding banking sector reforms by Narasmihan Committee were published in 1991 and 1998. These two reports made some recommendations to renders banking sectors firm and sound.

### 3.2.2 Scope of the Committee:

Scope of the committee is as follows:

1) To recommend measures for improvement in operational savings, functions and profitability of commercial banks and financial institutions in India.
2) To make recommendations for improvements in management policies and structural procedures.
3) To make recommendations regarding structure and adequacy of capital of banks.
4) To make recommendations to create competitive ability in Indian commercial banks and financial institutions.
5) To examine the existing legal framework and suggest improvements.
6) To recommend any suitable measures after their survey.

### 3.2.3 Recommendations of the Committee:

The Narasimhan Committee submitted its first report in 1991 and the second report in 1998 to Central Government. The total recommendation by the committee and their classification is as follows:

**A) Recommendations of the Committee Regarding Financial Management of Commercial Banks :**

1) Statutory liquidity ratio should be brought down to 25% from 97.5% in the next 5 years.
2) Cash Reserve Ratio should be brought down slowly to 5%.
3) Credit Supply schedule of commercial banks should follow the Directed Credit principle.
4) Controls over interest rates of banks should be relaxed or be removed.
5) Those loans on which there is no possibility of earning any interest should be considered as Non-Performing Assets.
6) Criteria should be finalised for country's interest income and interest on non-performing assets should not be counted. These loans which stop yielding any interest are called non-performing assets. This committee has classified non-performing assets into following four types :

**a) Standard Assets:**

Those assets on which there are satisfactory capital and interest repayments and there are no outstanding capital or interest dues are standard assets.

**b) Substandard Assets:**

Assets on which capital and interest are due for more than six months are substandard assets.

**c) Doubtful Assets:**

Assets for which capital and interest repayments are due for more than 2 years are doubtful assets.

**d) Loss Making Assets :**

Those assets which have been lying idle for more than 1 year are loss making assets.

**7)** Commercial Banks should follow a uniform accounting practice regarding calculation of income, classification of assets and bad debts.

**8)** There should be more transparency in balance sheets of banks and banks should disclose all important matters in accounts.

**9)** Separate courts should be established for loan recovery cases.

**10)** For bad debts and doubtful debts, An Asset Reconstruction Fund should be established.

**B) Recommendations Regarding Capital Structure of Commercial Banks :**

**1)** Capital Adequacy Norms should be applied to commercial banks. Capital adequacy ratio is the ratio of risk-loaded assets to capital. Such a ratio is recommended to be between 8 to 10% by the committee.

**2)** Permission should be granted to commercial banks to raise capital in the open market.

**3)** Capital should be provided considering market risks and credit risks.

**4)** Commercial banks should calculate Risk Assets Ratios.

**5)** Commercial banks should pay more attention to asset management.

**C) Recommendations Regarding Bank Business Structure :**

**1)** The entire banking system should be restructured. There should be 3 or 4 hours banks which can function on an international level. 8 to 10 banks should function at the national level. Remaining banks should work on rural and local levels.

**2)** One or two banks from public sector should try and set up independent rural banks for development of rural areas.

**3)** The procedure of licence for opening branches should be cancelled.

**4)** It should be declared that there should be no further bank nationalisation.

**5)** Permission should be granted to set up banks in the private sector.

**6)** Policy for opening branches by foreign banks in India should be relaxed.

**D) Recommendations Regarding Supervision of Bank Management:**

**1)** There should be an internal independent supervision authority within RBI to supervise commercial banks and financial institutions.

**2)** The present system comprising dual control i.e. controls by the banking department of the Central Government and that by RBI should come to an end and there should be regulation only by one authority.

**3)** The procedure for selection of CEO and Board of Directors of public sector banks should be amended.

**4)** Commercial banks should be supervised and inspected through international audit and inspection reports.

Government of India accepted most of the important recommendations of the Narasimhan Committee. However, it did not accept recommendations regarding restructuring of banks. Narasimhan Committee's recommendations were applied to Indian banking sector stage by stage.

## 3.2.4 Reforms of the Committee:

Attempts were made in 1969 to make fundamental changes in banking structure through nationalisation of banks. In 1991, restructuring of banking business as per Narasimhan Committee recommendation commenced with the objective of removing weak links in the banking system and implementation of bank policies consistent with new economic reforms. Some important recommendations of Narasimhan Committee which formed the basis of transformation and reforms in the banking industry need an explanation such as given below:

**1) Deregulation of Interest Rate:**

The Committee observed that the prevailing structure of administered rates was highly complex and rigid and called for deregulating it so that it reflects the emerging market conditions. However, it warned against instant deregulation and suggested that the rates be brought in line with the market rates gradually over a period of time. The Committee also recommended phasing out Concessional Interest rates

The Narasimhan Committee advocated that interest rates should be allowed to be determined by market forces. Since 1992, interest rates have become much simpler and freer.

**a)** Scheduled Commercial banks have now the freedom to set interest rates on their deposits subject to minimum floor rates and maximum ceiling rates.

**b)** Interest rate on domestic term deposits has been decontrolled.

**c)** The prime lending rate of SBI and other banks on general advances of over Rs. 2 lakhs has been reduced.

**d)** Rate of Interest on bank loans above Rs. 2 lakhs has been fully decontrolled.

**e)** The interest rates on deposits and advances of all Co-operative banks have been deregulated subject to a minimum lending rate of 13%.

**2) Cash Reserve Ratio (CRR):**

While making recommendations regarding financial management of commercial banks, Narasimhan committee explained the role of RBI policy concerning Cash Reserve Ratio and recommended that the RBI policy of keeping Cash Reserve Ratio at 15% should be brought down gradually to 5% in future.

**Definition:**

Cash Reserve Ratio means according to RBI Act, commercial banks should keep a specific acceptance of deposit income available with them and with RBI as their deposit. RBI has the authority to change Cash Reserve Ratio between 3 to 15%.

RBI seems to have consistently adopted the policy of increasing Cash Reserve Ratio as a means of quantitative credit control. RBI does not pay any interest on amount deposited with RBI as Cash Reserve Ratio. Reserve Bank frequently uses the policy of raising and lowering CRR and this affects profitability of commercial banks adversely. Commercial banks pay interest to depositors on their deposits and out of them; a large portion is kept with RBI which remain unproductive.

While analysing low profitability of commercial banks, Narasimhan Committee in their recommendation has stated that investments by banks should be made as per directions from RBI, for regulation of credit, instead of changing CRR, emphasis should be laid on sale / purchase of bonds in the open market and CRR should be brought down slowly to 5%.

**3) Statutory Liquidity Ratio (SLR) :**

In order to keep banking business healthy and credible economically, banks need to keep their assets in liquid form. Commercial banks accept deposits on the promise of payment on demand. Liquidity of banks is generally measured in terms of cash, gold, Government bonds, recognised securities, etc. As per Banking Regulation Act, RBI has authority to decide liquidity ratio of banks and to issue directors regarding liquidity. The ratios determined by RBI are called statutory Liquidity Ratios.

**Definition:**

Statutory Liquidity Ratio means the percentage decided by RBI that must be kept in terms of cash and Government securities out of their total deposit income by commercial banks.

RBI had increased Statutory Liquidity Ratio to 38.5%. Narasimhan committee had stated that the most important factor affecting profitability of commercial banks was Statutory Liquidity Ratio.

This was because commercial banks had to keep 15% Cash Reserve Ratio and Statutory Liquidity Ratio at 98.5%, thus, 53.5% of their deposit income with RBI, without interest, or with low interest or in terms of dividend and this affected profitability of banks. Narasimhan Committee recommended that Statutory Liquidity Ratio be brought to 25% in stages. This will result in more funds being available with commercial banks and these funds can be used for investment elsewhere which will increase profitability of commercial banks. Government of India has accepted this recommendation in principle and statutory liquidity ratio is being brought down in stages.

**4) Capital Adequacy Ratio:**

Recommendations by Narasimhan Committee regarding reforms in banking business, included recommendations regarding capital structure of banks with a view to have solid financial base for commercial banks and to have an adequate ratio between own funds of commercial banks and risk assets of banks (loans given by banks). Capital Adequacy Ratio is important.

**Definition:**

Capital Adequacy Ratio is the minimum ratio that should be kept between own funds of commercial banks and the loans issued by them or risk assets.

In India, Capital Adequacy Ratios are very low. This means that commercial banks consider that depositor's money is the main capital source and create loanable funds or risk assets through these deposits. If bank's own capital is for less compared to its turnover, it becomes an obstacle in the healthy growth of the bank.

According to Narasimhan Committee, there can be 4 groups of commercial banks on the basis of capital adequacy ratio.

**a)** Banks with less than 4% as Capital Adequacy Ratio.

**b)** Capital Adequacy Ratio 4 to 8%.

**c)** Capital Adequacy Ratio 8 to 10% and

**d)** Capital Adequacy Ratio 10% or more.

Narasimhan Committee has recommended that RBI should keep at least 8% Capital Adequacy Ratio as the norm for each bank and it should be made obligatory to all banks to declare their Capital Adequacy Ratios to RBI and other shareholders. This recommendation of Narasimhan Committee was accepted by Government of India.

**5) Interest Rate structure:**

After independence, a policy of regulated interest rates was adopted with help from RBI. It was obligatory for commercial banks to decide interest rates on deposits, various term loans and other reasons such as - agricultural credit, consumer credit, etc. as per instructions from RBI.

Narasimhan Committee recommended cancellation of interest policy under the control of RBI. According to this committee, in future, policy of interest rates should be market oriented. This means that interest rates should be decided through balancing of supply and demand of loanable funds. Commercial banks should be free to decide interest rates for deposits and loans. It stated that if interest rates on banking sector are made free of controls, monetary market will be more active and economic, industrial and structural development will be more dynamic because of favourable atmosphere for capital investments through competitive interest rates. RBI should use Bank Rate only as a supporting mechanism. Changes in Bank Rate should be used for adoption of monetary and credit control policies.

**6) Directed Credit Programme:**

Directed Credit Programme was undertaken in order to bring about quick and balanced developments. Those economic sectors which were deprived of development were included in priority sectors. In this small and border line farmers, farm, labour, rural industries, cottage industries, families below poverty line, agricultural sector, small industries, transport, etc. are included. RBI directs commercial banks to provide loans at discounted rates to this sector which was deprived from development or neglected. According to RBI, it was mandatory for commercial banks to provide a total of 41% loans at low interest rates which included 40% for priority sectors and one per cent for families below poverty line. Such policies over a long term were affecting profitability of commercial banks. At the same time, it was useful for development of priority sector.

Narasimhan Committee made a recommendation that directed credit programme should be gradually slowed down and Government should implement treasury measures because treasury measures of Central Government are more effective than directions issued to banks regarding loans to rejected or priority sectors. According to Narasimhan Committee, priority sectors should include only limited areas such as borderline farmers, rural artisans, rural and cottage industries only. RBI should give necessary directions for credit supply to these sectors. 10% finance should be given through directors and a re-examination should be done whether such provision should be kept for next 3 years or not. For the 10% finance issued under directives, supervision, technical and financial screening is essential and there should not be any political, administrative or judicial interference in this matter.

**7) Income Recognition and Asset Classification:**

While making recommendations on financial management of commercial banks, Narasimhan Committee has made some suggestions regarding Income Recognition and Asset Classification while deciding criteria for computing interest income.

**a) Income Computation:**

Commercial banks were given clear explanation regarding "Income Recognition and Asset Classification" so that they are clear what types of interest on loans can be considered as a source in their balance sheets. RBI gave instructions to commercial banks to follow a common accounting method for income computation, asset classification and bad debts.

According to Health Codes method those risk loaded assets and interest thereon, is outstanding upto maximum 6 months can be included in the balance sheet. However, those risk assets where interest and capital repayments are outstanding over 6 months' i. e. doubtful assets and loss assets cannot be computed as interest income in balance sheets.

Above rules were made mandatory for all banks in India for Income Recognition and Asset Classification. It was also made obligatory to submit statements of accounts in the format decided by RBI.

**b) Asset Classification:**

Narasimhan Committee put forward some logical criteria for assets considering loan accounts of commercial banks and health code number determined for income competition. Loan accounts of commercial banks and transactions of interests and capital repayment on such loan account form the basis of assets classification as follows:

i) **Standard Assets:**

Those assets on which interest and capital installments are not outstanding or in other words those loans for which there is satisfactory interest and loan repayments are called standard assets.

ii) **Sub-standard Assets :**

Those loans for which interest and capital repayment is outstanding for more than six months are called sub-standard assets.

iii) **Doubtful Assets:**

Those loans for which interest and repayments are overdue for more than two years are called doubtful assets.

iv) **Loss Assets:**

Those loans on which interest and capital repayments are outstanding for more than three years i.e. recovery for which has proved difficult but which are still not written off are considered as loss assets.

Narasimhan Committee has included assets number 2 to number 4 in the above list i.e. substandard, doubtful and loss assets as non-performing assets. It recommended that until interest on non-performing is actually realised, it should not be considered as income in the balance sheet. Government of India accepted this recommendation and implemented the recommendation regarding 'income recognition and asset classification' for banking business in 1994.

8) **Provisioning Norms:**

While recommending measures for financial management of bank, Narasimhan Committee determined Health Codes regarding all kinds of advances or loans given by commercial banks, for computing interest on such loans in respect of total loan and interest portfolio of commercial banks. These are also called as common norms for provision of loans by commercial banks. This committee has determined following eight types of Health Codes for classification of bank loan:

| Health Code No. | State of Loan Account |
|---|---|
| 1 | Satisfactory |
| 2 | Irregular |
| 3 | Sick but economically viable loans |
| 4 | Sick but non-viable |
| 5 | Loans for which repayments can be demanded |
| 6 | Loans in court cases |
| 7 | Loans which are sold |
| 8 | Bad debts |

According to Health codes which show provision of norms concerning loan accounts clear instructions were given that until interest on loans indicated against 5 to 8 health codes is actually realised. The interest income on such account should not be considered as income in balance sheets. RBI has accepted above health codes and made this rule mandatory for commercial banks while preparing their accounts.

**9) Redefining of the NPAs :**

A non-performing asset is defined as a credit facility in respect of which the interest and/or instalments of principal has remained 'over-due' for a specified length of time. When recommending financial liberalisation as a solution to the "problem" of low profitability, there was the immediate problem of dealing with the existing large element of non-performing assets (NPAs) in banks' portfolio. Subjecting banks that had hitherto functioned under a completely different discipline to market-based competition and the threat of closure would have amounted to discrimination vis-a-vis new entrants with adequate resources.

The Narasimham Committee coined a new definition of NPAs, in conformity with the international practice. From 1991-92, banks had to classify their advances into four groups:

**(i)** Standard assets. **(ii)** Sub-standard assets, **(iii)** doubtful assets, and **(iv)** loss assets; and indicated that the advances classified under the last three groups were to be considered as NPAs.

However, the argument of high NPAs was used to encourage banks to cut back on lending to the priority sector. Among the directed credit programmes followed by the banks, the priority sector lending has been perhaps one of the most effective.

**10) Management of Non-Performing Accounts:**

Out of many recommendations regarding banking business reforms by Narasimhan Committee, determination of non-performing assets and provision for management of such assets are especially important recommendations.

Those loan accounts for which interest and capital repayments are outstanding for more than six months, are called non-performing assets. In 1998, the committee recommended an amendment in this provision so as to consider loans with outstanding for more than 90 days as non-performing assets. Commercial banks should be classified according to proportion of non-performing assets that are decided with the help of health codes and assets classification.

**a)** Banks with NPA up to 10%

**b)** Banks with NPA 10 to 20%

**c)** Banks with NPA more than 20%

Banks in second and third groups should make efforts to bring down NPA to less than 10%. The 1998 recommendation stated that by the year 2002, all commercial banks should bring down their NPA to less than 5%. The committee recommended following measures for management of NPAs of commercial banks:

**i)** Commercial banks should make a provision of 10% of their profit for recovery of substandard assets.

**ii)** They should provide 20% of profit for recovery at doubtful assets.

**iij)** Bank should provide 100% for recovery of loss assets out of their profit.

Thus, the committee recommended keeping aside a certain percentage of profits for making up the loss sustained by banks against NPA.

Narasimhan Committee had accepted recommendations of the earlier Tiwari Committee and stated that a separate court be established for recovery of non-performing loans. Such courts should handle only NPA cases and speed up loan recovery and actions.

The committee recommended setting up an 'Assets Reconstruction Funds'. Government of India, RBI, Public sector banks and financial institutions should take initiative in establishment of ARF. These funds should offer their own bonds for sale and should even pay interest. At the same time doubtful and loss assets of different banks and financial institutions should be transferred to these funds. The funds should activate the necessary process for recovery of NPAs and should appoint an expert committee. This committee should take suitable decisions. Once recovery of NPAs is achieved, payable of ARFs will be made through these funds. And once the recovery is complete, the same fund will cease to exist having accomplished its objective.

In short, various provisions such as every bank should keep aside a certain portion of its profit income for NPAs, setting up of special courts and establishment of ARF for the purpose of management of NPAs.

**11) Special Tribunals for Recovery of Loans :**

Tiwari Committee has recommended that special tribunal should be set up for recovery of dues of banks and financial institutions in order to resolve the problem of outstanding loans in a legal manner. Narasimhan Committee upheld Tiwari Committee's suggestions and recommended establishment of special tribunals for recovery while stating the provisions for bank reforms. According to Narasimhan Committee recovery cases are kept pending in civil court for very long periods. Hence, the question of outstanding is becoming more and more difficult to find the way out of this problem, special tribunals for loan recovery would be useful. This will speed up court decisions and the questions of NPA will become less serious.

According to Narasimhan Committee's recommendations, Government of India passed the 1993 Loan Recovery Act. As per this law, RBI set up loan recovery tribunals in eight large cities in 1995 and RBI has decided to set up 20 more such tribunals in future. Besides, an Appellate Tribunal is set up at Mumbai Recommendations by Narasimhan Committee, and response by Government of India and RBI to these recommendations has ensured that in future loan recovery cases will be resolved faster in future.

**12) Structure of Banking System:**

In order that banking operations became more flexible and banks set internal autonomy, the present structure of banking business or its profile is not found very suitable considering nature of Indian economy and geographical vastness, it is necessary to bring about a remarkable change in the banking system or procedural profile. Considering that bank employees must be taken into confidence while changing the structure and considering bank's objectives and profit motive, the committee made some important recommendations.

**a)** State Bank of India and some public sector banks need to expand their functions in the international areas. Therefore, some public sector banks should be brought together so that 3 to 4 banks are given the functions of international business and expansion. If 3 to 4 Public Banks and State Bank come together and form some very large banks, their competitive strength will be a greater and they will be able to create a network of banking services on the national and international level.

**b)** 8 to 10 banks on the national level are set up through consolidation and mergers of banks. These banks should be able to spread the network of branches throughout the country and should be able to perform some wider duties.

**c)** Considering geographical expense of India, a structure of banking business based on local situation and having regional jurisdiction is required. Except above banks, all other banks in India should be of local or regional nature.

**d)** Regional rural banks and co-operative banks have their jurisdiction in rural areas. These banks should perform the functions of providing banking services for agriculture related industry, agriculture and rural economy considering the local requirements of rural economic system.

**e)** Government should declare that banks will not be nationalised in future. Permission should be given to set up private banks. However a capital of base Rs. 100 crores should be specified Public sector banks and private banks should be treated on par.

**f)** Narasimhan Committee recommended that Government should allow foreign banks to open offices in India and set up subsidiary banks. Foreign banks should respect economic and social responsibilities as Indian banks do and permission may be granted to foreign and Indian banks to set up banks in India taking joint risk.

**g)** If the above structure of banks cause some shortcomings in regional or sector wise banking services, new local area banks should be allowed to be set up to fill any gaps. These LAB (Local Area) Banks should be allotted specific geographical areas.

**13) Supervision of Banks:**

Banks have a unique place in the economic structure and life of every country. It is essential that interests of depositors and bank customers be taken into consideration. It is important to have to see whether banks take care of depositor's interest while using depositor's money for the progress of their businesses and hence, supervision of banks and provisions thereof are important. Objectives of supervision department are to see how much risk banks undertake and how much risk they are capable of bearing. The supervision committee has various jobs such as following:

Whether commercial banks are performing according to their objectives and working under Banking Regulation Act, whether policies of commercial banks are considered with banking business norms, how much risk banks undertake and which risks can cause harm to bank, etc.

In order to enhance the credibility of banking sector, Narasimhan Committee made following recommendations regarding supervision of banks:

**a)** An independent supervision authority should be established within RBI to supervise banks and financial institutions.

**b)** Dual control on banks should end and banking system should be brought under the control of Government Banking Department or RBI, any one of the two authorities.

**c)** Methods of selections of CEOs and Boards of Directors of public banks should be improved.

**d)** Internal audit and inspection report should be major means of supervision.

The Central Government accepted recommendation of the committee regarding the supervision. RBI set up a financial supervision board in May 1993. This board was given the responsibility of control over credit supply by commercial bank, asset classification income recognition, adequacy of capital and treasury operations. The Governor of RBI is Chairman of this board.

Reserve Bank set up an independent supervision board in December 1992. This board was given the responsibility of supervising day-to-day operations of commercial banks and non-banking financial institutions. Besides above broad recommendations by Narasimhan Committee regarding banking reforms in 1991, many other provisions regarding improvements in banking were put forward.

**CAMEL**

C = Capital

A = Assets

M = Management

E = Earning

L = Liquidity

Many improvements were included regarding CAMEL rating, asset management method compromise regarding loan recoveries establishment of consultative committees, computerised inspection, etc. In short, in the decade of 1990s, various policies were adopted to totally transform the Indian banking business. Bank-reform provisions, thus, have performed the function of making Indian banking sector more alert to face open competition.

## 3.3 Narsimhan Committee - II:

The Narasimhan Committee (II) was constituted to take the review of structure, organisation, functions and procedures of the financial system in India with reference to the banking progress. The committee submitted its report in November 1991. It made close observations of the banking and financial system in India and suggested certain recommendations. These suggestions are made applicable by the government to the banking system in a successful manner.

The progress already made in the reform of the financial sector is a substantial and has generated confidence in the banking sector. In this background, a committee on banking sector reforms (the second Narasimhan Committee) was constituted. This committee submitted its report in April, 1998.

### 3.3.1 Recommendations:

The recommendations are as follows:

**A) Consolidation of Banking System:**

**1) Finding Out Weak Banks :**

Here 'weak banks' means that banker which has a potential for development but there is some problems or deficiencies in its operational system. So the financial, operational and organisational restructuring should be undertaken with respect to such banks. A 'weak bank' should be a banking institution whose accumulated losses and net NPAs exceed its net worth or one whose operating profits less its income on recapitalisation bonds is negative for three consecutive years.

**2) Mergers of Two Banks / Institutions:**

Merging of 'one weak bank' with other well settled bank is not the solution of the problem of weak bank. Before merging, there are some factors which should be taken into account for the future stability and profitability of such mergers:

i) There should be operational and organisational similarity between the two institutions.

ii) The operating area i. e. location of the institutions.

iii) Business complementary that is the functions and objectives of both the institutions should be supportive to one another.

So merger can be done between two banks. Bank and DFIs (Development Financial Institutions), bank and NBFCs (Non-banking Financial Corporations).

**3) Joint Ventures :**

Foreign banks be allowed to set up subsidiaries / joint ventures and there are treated at par with other private banks.

**B) Directed Credit Programme :**

Directed Credit Programmes have played a useful role in extending the reach of the banking system to cover sectors which were neglected hitherto. Despite considerable unproductive lending, there is evidence that the contribution of bank credit to the growth of agriculture and small industry has made an impact. Many sectors are now able to stand on their own fact, this call for some re-examination of the present relevance of directed credit programmes.

Accordingly, directed credit programmes should be phased out and priority sector should be redefined. The credit target for this redefined priority sector should be fixed at 10 per cent of aggregate credit.

**C) Redefining of NPAs (Non - performing Assets):**

a) Government guaranteed advances which have turned sticky to be classified as NPAs.

b) Banks with high NPA portfolio, loan assets in the doubtful and loss categories are transferred to an "Asset Reconstruction Company" (ARC). Asset Reconstruction Company to issue NPA swap bonds representing the realisable value of the asset transferred.

c) Distinction is made between NPAs arising out of reasons which are client specific and institution, specific and general factors such as agro, climatic and environmental issues.

d) An independent loan review mechanism is instituted especially for large borrower's accounts and to identify potential NPAs.

e) Banks to reduce the average level of net NPAs to less than 5 per cent by the year 2000 and 3 per cent by 2002. In the case of banks with international presence, the minimum objective should be to reduce net NPAs to 3 percent and nil by these dates.

**D) Revision in the Capital Adequacy:**

a) Capital adequacy requirements to take into consideration market risks in addition to credit risks.

b) Recapitalisation of banks from the government budget is discontinued forthwith.

c) In respect of those banks whose operations have been profitable and which enjoy a good reputation in the markets, could approach the capital market for enhancement of their capital.

d) Before arriving at the capital adequacy ratio for each bank, it is necessary that the assets of the banks be evaluated on the basis of their realised values.

## 3.4 Banking Reforms Measures:

The Committee on the Financial System (1991) had observed that the Indian Banking System have made appreciable progress in having geographical reach and functional strength. Inspite of this commendable progress, several issues had emerged which had resulted in decline of productivity, efficiency and erosion of profitability of the Banking Sector. Social Banking agenda of the Government had made most of the PSBs unprofitable. The Narasimham Committee had described the reasons as:

**a)** Meeting the SLR and CRR obligations by the Banks.

**b)** Directed credit disbursement through Priority Sector lending.

Interest rate regime was rigid and complex followed by inadequacy of capital requirements and faulty income recognition, asset classification and provisioning norms. The Banks' Balance Sheet did not reflect their true health since income was recognized on accrual basis resulting in reporting of inflated profits. Quantitative restrictions for credit squeeze/rationing coupled with regulated interest regime had led to sub optimal use of credit resulting in low level of investments and thus lower economic growth.

All this finally resulted into the financial repression which ultimately led to decline in productivity, efficiency and erosion of the profitability of the Indian Banks.

## 3.4.1 Cash Reserve Ratio (C.R.R.) and Statutory Liquidity Ratio (S.L.R):

One of the primary functions of Reserve Bank of India (RBI) is to control the supply of money in the economy and also 'the cost of credit.' Meaning, how much money is available for the industry or the economy and what is the price that the economy has to pay to borrow that money. 'Availability of money' is nothing but liquidity and 'cost of borrowing' is interest rates these two things (Supply of money and cost of credit) are closely monitored and controlled by RBI. These two factors will have considerable impact on inflation and growth. To control inflation and the growth, RBI uses certain tools like Cash Reserve Ratio, Statutory Liquidity Ratio, Repo Rate, Reverse Repo Rate etc.

**A) Cash Reserve Ratio:**

Cash Reserve Ratio (CRR) is the share of a bank's total deposit that is mandated by the Reserve Bank of India (RBI) to be maintained with the latter in the form of liquid cash. The Cash Reserve Ratio acts as one of the reference rates when determining the base rate. Base rate means the minimum lending rate below which a bank is not allowed to lend funds. The base rate is determined by the Reserve Bank of India (RBI). The rate is fixed and ensures transparency with respect to borrowing and lending in the credit market. The Base Rate also helps the banks to cut down on their cost of lending to be able to extend affordable loans. As per the RBI guidelines, every bank is required to maintain a ratio of their total deposits that can also be held with currency chests. This is considered to be the same as it is kept with the RBI. The RBI can change this ratio from time to time in regular intervals. When this ratio is changed, it impacts the economy. For banks, profits are made by lending. In pursuit of this goal, banks may lend out to the max to make higher profits and have very less cash with them. An unexpected rush by customers to withdraw their deposits will lead to banks being unable to meet all the repayment needs. Therefore, CRR is vital to ensure that there is always a certain fraction of all the deposits in every bank, kept safe with them. RBI curbs these issues with the help of the CRR.

**B) Statutory Liquidity Ratio:**

Statutory Liquidity Ratio or SLR is a minimum percentage of deposits that a commercial bank has to maintain in the form of liquid cash, gold or other securities. It is basically the reserve requirement that banks is expected to keep before offering credit to customers. These are not reserved with the Reserve Bank of India (RBI), but with banks themselves. The SLR is fixed by the RBI. CRR (Cash Reserve Ratio) and SLR have been the traditional tools of the central bank's monetary policy to control credit growth, flow of liquidity and inflation in the economy. The SLR was prescribed by Section 24 (2A) of Banking Regulation Act, 1949.

**C) Reduced Dependency on CRR and SLR:**

In consonance with the medium-term objectives of the financial sector reform, the SLR was brought down drastically. Moreover, there were sharp cuts in the CRR. The Narasimhan committee recommended that RBI should increasingly rely on Open Market Operations (OMOs) and reduce its dependence on CRR. As a result, the CRR, which was 15 per cent in 1991-92, was reduced to 4.75 per cent in 2003-04. The SLR provision has created a captive market for the government securities which increases automatically with the growth in the liabilities of banks. The base SLR that stood at 38.5 per cent in 1990-91 has come down to a uniform level of 25 per cent from 1997-98 onwards. It suggests that these reductions will have implications on the availability of Hinds with banks for lending. It is, however, an irony that even though the SLR was reduced to help banks. The banks continue to voluntarily maintain the SLR securities worth more than 25 per cent (in case of some banks, more than 40 per cent) as the interest rates on government securities became competitive without the associated risk. The RBI's refinance facility was also rationalized while lowering the CRR-the sector specific refinance Facilities were de-emphasized and simultaneously a general refinance window was opened in April 1997.

**Table No.: 3.1: Movements in CRR, SLR and Bank Rate**

| Year | CRR | SLR | Bank Rate |
|---|---|---|---|
| **1991-92** | 15 | 38.5 | 10 |
| **1992-93** | 15 | 38.5 | 12 |
| **1993-94** | 15 | 37.25 | 12 |
| **1994-95** | 14 | 34.75 | 12 |
| **1995-96** | 15 | 33.75 | 12 |
| **1996-97** | 14 | 33.75 | 12 |
| **1997-98** | 10 | 33.75 | 9 |
| **1998-99** | 9.50 | 25 | 8 |
| **1999-2000** | 9 | 25 | 7 |

| | | | |
|---|---|---|---|
| **2000-01** | 5 | 25 | 6.5 |
| **2001-02** | 4.75 | 25 | 6.25 |
| **2002-03** | 4.50 | 25 | 6 |
| **2003-04** | 4.75 | 25 | 6 |

Along with a reduction in the CRR and SLR, the bank rate also met with a decline to which all other rates are aligned, but only after 1997. The bank rate is the rate at which a bank is prepared to buy or rediscount bills of exchange or other Commercial Papers (CPs) eligible under the RBI Act. In the pre-reform period, the role for the bank rate was limited in the monetary policy and was not subjected to many changes. However, since 1997-98, it was reactivated as the signaling and reference rate. All interest rates on the RBI advances and penal interest rates on shortfalls in reserve requirements have been linked to the bank rate as has been the interest rates on other categories of accommodation. It helps to develop an inter-bank term market giving rise to a signalling and reference rate. Between 1997-98 and 2003-04, the bank rate has changed substantially. However, since liquidity is being provided at reverse repo rate, as and when required importance of the bank rate as a signaling rate has declined. Since 2003-2004, the bank rate remained unchanged.

### 3.4.2 Prudential Norms:

Prudential regulation refers to a set of laws and rules designed to minimise the risks banks assume and to ensure the safety and soundness of both individual institutions and the system as a whole. Banks are advised not to enter into swap transactions involving conversion of fixed rate rupee liabilities in respect of Innovative Tier I/Tier II bonds into floating rate foreign currency liabilities. Banks are required to maintain a minimum CRAR of 9 per cent on an ongoing basis.

There are two types of banking regulation-economic and prudential. In the pre-reform era (before July 1991) the Reserve Bank of India (RBI) regulated banks by imposing constraints on interest rates, tightening entry norms and directed lending to ensure judicious end use of bank credit.

However, such economic regulation of banks hampered their productivity and efficiency. Hence, the RBI switched over to prudential regulation which calls for imposing minimum limit on the capital level(s) of banks.

The objective is to maintain the wealth of banks in particular and to ensure the soundness of the financial system in general. It allows much greater scope for the free play of market forces than what is permitted by economic regulations alone.

On the basis of recommendations of the Committee on Banking Sector Reforms, April 1998 (the second Narasimhan Committee) the RBI issued prudential norms. The major objective of setting such norms was to ensure financial safety, soundness and solvency of banks. These norms are directed toward ensuring that banks carry on their operations as prudent entities, are free from undue risk-taking, and do not violate banking regulations in pursuit of profit. The main focus of reforms was in three areas:

**1) Non-Performing Assets (NPAs):**

One serious problem faced by the public sector banks in the 1990s was a high proportion of NPAs. An NPA is an asset from which income is overdue for more than six months. According to the second Narasimhan Committee report (1998), "No other single indicator reflects the quality of assets and their impact on banks' viability than the NPA figures in relation to advances."

The gross NPAs of scheduled commercial banks (SCBs) increased over the period March 31, 1998 to March 31, 2002 from Rs 50,815 crores to Rs 70,904 crores. Gross NPA of public sector banks (PSBs) were also correspondingly higher. However, the share of PSBs in total NPAs declined from 90% to 80% during the period (1998-2002).

Furthermore, there was a decline in the ratio of gross NPAs and net NPAs, measured as percentage of advances as well as assets. These ratios represent the quality of banks assets and are thus taken as measures of soundness of the banking system. Gross and net NPAs as a proportion of gross advances and total assets of SCBs declined substantially during this period.

However, the ratio of gross and net NPAs as a proportion of gross advances and of total assets increased substantially for new private sector banks from 2001-02 due to the merger of strong banks with weak banks.

But the root cause of increase in NPAs is the increasing proportion of bad debt. In case of some banks, net NPAs even exceeded their net worth. This means that such banks had negative net worth. The RBI offered three options to banks to restructure bad debts:

**a)** Debt Recovery Tribunals (DRTs)

**b)** Settlement Advisory Committees (SACs)

**c)** Recapitalisation from the Government

Guidelines on SACs were revised in July 2002 to provide a uniform, simplified, non-discriminatory and non-discretionary mechanism for the recovery of the stock of NPAs of all banks. Altogether, seven DRTs have been set up for speedy recovery of loans. Finally with a view to enhancing the effectiveness of DRTs, the Central government amended the Recovery of Debts due to Banks and Financial Institutions Act in Jan, 2002.

**2) Capital Adequacy Norms/ Ratio:**

Capital Adequacy Ratio (CAR) is the ratio of a bank's capital in relation to its risk weighted assets and current liabilities. However, as per RBI norms, Indian scheduled commercial banks are required to maintain of CAR of 9% while Indian public sector banks are emphasized to maintain a CAR of 12%. The capital adequacy ratio ((CAR) measures the amount of capital a bank retains compared to its risk. The CAR is important to shareholders because it is an important measure of the financial soundness of a bank.

Banking sector reforms were initiated by implementing prudential norms consisting of Capital Adequacy Ratio (CAR). The core of such reforms has been the broadening of prudential norms to the internationally accepted standards.

In 1988 the Basle Committee for international banking supervision made an attempt worldwide to reduce the number of bank failures by tying a bank's CAR to the riskiness of the loans it makes. For instance, there is less chance of a loan to a government going bad than a loan to, say, an internet business. So, the bank will not have to hold as much capital in reserve against the first loan as against the second.

Throughout the world, commercial banks are under the legal obligation to maintain minimum capital funds for the sake of safety. The reason is that a bank's capital base is vitally important for its long-term variability. It also acts as a shock absorber in the medium term since it gives the power to absorb shocks and thus avoid the risk of bankruptcy.

A bank's capital funds must be equivalent to the prescribed ratio on the aggregate of the risk weighted assets and other exposures. CAR is a measure of the amount of a bank's capital expressed as a percentage of its risk weighted credit exposures. It is related to risk weight assigned to asset acquired by banks in the normal process of conducting business. It is also related to the proportion of capital to be maintained on such aggregate risk weighted assets.

CAR is calculated on the basis of risk weightage on assets in the books of accounts of banks. Any type of business transaction carried out by a bank involves a certain specific type of risk. So, for the sake of safety, a portion of capital has to be set aside to make provision for this risk. This portion acts as a hedge against uncertainty, i.e., a 'secret reserve' to absorb any possible future loss. Higher Capital Adequacy will improve the efficiency of banks in two ways:

**a)** By forcing banks to reduce operating costs.

**b)** By improving long-term viability through risk reduction.

Capital adequacy enables banks to mobilise more capital at reasonable cost.

The two important new parameters which are crucial for the growth of banks are asset quality and risk weightage.

### 3.4.3 Credit Deposit Ratio (C. D. Ratio):

Credit-deposit ratio, popularly CD ratio, is the ratio of how much a bank lends out of the deposits it has mobilized. RBI does not stipulate a minimum or maximum level for the ratio, but a very low ratio indicates banks are not making full use of their resources.

## 3.5 Framework of Basel Committees on Banking Supervision:

A New Standard for the Measurement of Risks in Banks, and for the Allocation of Capital to cover those risks, published by the Basel Committee of G10 Central Banks. Basel Committee performs following functions:

**1)** Acts as Think-Tank for banking regulators.

**2)** Issues guidance on best practice for banks.

**3)** Standards accepted worldwide.

**4)** Generally incorporated in national banking regulations.

### 3.5.1 Basel - I:

Basel is a city in Switzerland. It is the headquarters of Bureau of International Settlement (BIS), which fosters co-operation among central banks with a common goal of financial stability and common standards of banking regulations. Every two months BIS hosts a meeting of the governor and senior officials of central banks of member countries. Currently there are 27 member nations in the committee. Basel guidelines refer to broad supervisory standards formulated by this group of central banks - called the Basel Committee on Banking Supervision (BCBS). The set of agreement by the BCBS, which mainly focuses on risks to banks and the financial system are called Basel accord. The purpose of the accord is to ensure that financial institutions have enough capital on account to meet obligations and absorb unexpected losses. India has accepted Basel accords for the banking system. In fact, on a few parameters the RBI has prescribed stringent norms as compared to the norms prescribed by BCBS.

Basel I, that is, the 1988 Basel Accord, is primarily focused on credit risk and appropriate risk-weighting of assets. Assets of banks were classified and grouped in five categories according to credit risk, carrying risk weights of 0% (for example cash, bullion, home country debt like Treasuries), 20% (securitisations such as mortgage-backed securities (MBS) with the highest AAA rating) 50%, 100% (for example, most corporate debt), and some assets given No rating. Banks with an international presence are required to hold capital equal to 8% of their risk-weighted assets (RWA).

**The tier 1 capital ratio = tier 1 capital / all RWA**

**The total capital ratio = (tier 1 + tier 2 + tier 3 capital) / all RWA**

**Leverage ratio = total capital/average total assets**

Banks are also required to report off-balance-sheet items such as letters of credit, unused commitments, and derivatives. These all factor into the risk weighted assets. The report is typically submitted to the Federal Reserve Bank as HC-R for the bank-holding company and submitted to the OCC as RC-R for just the bank.

### 3.5.2 Basel - II:

In response to the banking crises of the 1990s and the aforementioned criticisms of Basel I, the Basel Committee decided in 1999 to propose a new, more comprehensive capital adequacy accord. This accord, known formally as A Revised Framework on International Convergence of Capital Measurement and Capital Standards and informally as "Basel II" greatly expands the scope, technicality, and depth of the original Basel Accord. While maintaining the "pillar" framework of Basel I, each pillar is greatly expanded in Basel II to cover new approaches to credit risk, adapt to the securitization of bank assets, cover market, operational, and interest rate risk, and incorporate market based surveillance and regulation.

**1) Pillar 1- Minimum Capital Requirements:**

The first "pillar," known again as Minimum Capital Requirements, shows the greatest amount of expansion since Basel I. In response to Basel I's critics, Basel II creates a more sensitive measurement of a bank's risk-weighted assets and tries to eliminate the loopholes in Basel I that allow banks to take on additional risk while cosmetically assuaging to minimum capital adequacy requirements. Its first mandate is to broaden the scope of regulation to include assets of the holding company of an internationally active bank. This is done to avoid the risk that a bank will "hide" risk-taking by transferring its assets to other subsidiaries and also to incorporate the financial health of the entire firm in the calculation of capital requirements for its subsidiary bank.

**a) Credit Risk-the Standardized Approach :**

Next, the first "pillar" provides three methodologies to rate the riskiness of a bank's assets. The first of these methodologies, the "standardized" approach, extends the approach to capital weights used in Basel I to include market-based rating agencies. Sovereign claims, instead of being discounted according to the participation of the sovereign in the OECD, are now discounted according to the credit rating assigned to a sovereign's debt by an "authorized" rating institution-if debt is rated from AAA to AAA-, it is assigned a 0% weight; if it is rated from A+ to A-, it is assigned a 20% weight; if it is rated from BBB+ to BBB-, it receives a 50% weight; if it is rated from BB+ to BB-, it receives a 100% weight; and if it is rated below B-, it receives a 150% weight. Unrated debt is weighted at 100%. If a debt is denominated and funded in local currency, regulators can also assign a lower weight to its relative riskiness. In the "standard" approach, corporate debt is weighted in the same manner as bank debt, except the 100% category is extended to include all debt that is rated between BBB+ and BB-. All debt rated below BB-is weighted at 150%; unrated debt is risk-weighted at 100%. Home mortgages are, in addition, risk-weighted at 35%, while corporate mortgages are weighted at 100%.

**b) Credit Risk-Internal Ratings Based Approach :**

Beyond the "standardized" approach, Basel II proposes and incentivizes two alternate approaches toward risk-weighting capital, each known as an Internal Ratings Based Approach, or IRB. These approaches encourage banks to create their own internal systems to rate risk with the help of regulators. By forcing banks to "scale up" their risk-weighted reserves by 6% if they use the standardized approach, the Basel Committee offers banks the possibility of lower reserve holdings and thus higher profitability if they adopt these internal approaches.

**i) Foundation of IRB Approach :**

The first internal ratings based approach is known as the Foundation IRB. In this approach, banks, with the approval of regulators, can develop probability of default models that provide in-house risk weightings for their loan books. Regulators provide the "assumptions" in these models, namely the probability of loss of each type of asset, the exposure of a bank to an at-risk asset at the time of its default, and the maturity risk associated with each type of asset.

**ii) Advanced IRB Approach :**

The second internal ratings based approach, Advanced IRB, is essentially the same as Foundation IRB, except for one important difference: the banks themselves rather than regulators determine the assumptions of proprietary credit default models. Therefore, only the largest banks with the most complex modes can use this standard.

**iii) Operational Risks**

Basel II extends its scope into the assessment of and protection against operational risks. To calculate the reserves needed to adequately guard against failures in internal processes, the decision-making of individuals, equipment, and other external events, Basel II proposes three mutually exclusive methods.

**I) Basic Indicator Approach :**

The first method, known as the Basic Indicator Approach, recommends that banks hold capital equal to fifteen percent of the average gross income earned by a bank in the past three years. Regulators are allowed to adjust the 15% number according to their risk assessment of each bank.

**II) Standardized Approach :**

The second method, known as the Standardized Approach, divides a bank by its business lines to determine the amount of cash it must have on hand to protect itself against operational risk. Each line is weighted by its relative size within the company to create the percentage of assets the bank must hold. Figure below displays the reserves targets by business line. As shown below, less operationally risky business lines such as retail banking have lower reserve targets, while more variable and risky business lines such as corporate finance have higher targets.

**III) Advanced Measurement Approach :**

The third method, the Advanced Measurement Approach, is much less arbitrary than its rival methodologies. On the other hand, it is much more demanding for regulators and banks alike. It allows banks to develop their own reserve calculations for operational risks. Regulators, of course, must approve the final results of these models. This approach, much like the IRB approaches shown in the last section, is an attempt to bring market discipline and self-surveillance into banking legislation and a move to eliminate "wiggle room" where banks obey regulations in rule but not in spirit.

**IV) Market Risk :**

The last risk evaluated in Pillar I of the Basel II accords attempts to quantify the reserves needed to be held by banks due to market risk, i.e. the risk of loss due to movements in asset prices. In its evaluation of market risk, Basel II makes a clear distinction between fixed income and other products such as equity, commodity, and foreign exchange vehicles and also separates the two principal risks that contribute to overall market risk: interest rate and volatility risk. For fixed income assets, a proprietary risk measurement called "value at risk" (VAR) is first proposed alongside the lines of the IRB approaches and the Advanced Measurement Approach; banks can develop their own calculations to determine the reserves needed to protect against interest rate and volatility risk for fixed income assets on a position-by-position basis. Again, regulators must approve of such an action.

**2) Pillars II: Regulator Bank Interaction:**

Pillars II and III are much less complex and lengthy than Pillar I, they only occupy 40 of the 350 pages of the Basel II Accord. Pillar II primarily addresses regulator-bank interaction, extending the rights of the regulator in bank supervision and dissolution. Regulators are given the power to oversee the internal risk evaluation regimes proposed in Pillar-I and change them to the simpler, more conservative "bucket-based" approaches if they deem a bank unable to manage its credit, market, and operational risks independently. Regulators can also review a bank's capital assessment policy when they see fit, and are given the mandate to hold senior management responsible if a bank misrepresents its risk positioning. Moreover, banks are charged with drafting their own risk profiles, and if this reporting is not done, authorities have the right to penalize the at-fault bank. Two additional mandates also widen the breath of regulator power in Basel II. Firstly, regulators are allowed to create a "buffer" capital requirement in addition to the minimum capital requirements as calculated in Pillar I if banks are seen to be "skirting" around the capital adequacy goals of the accord. Secondly, to avoid a repeat of the financial crises in countries like Korea and China, banking supervisors are urged to mandate early action if capital reserves fall below minimum levels and are given significant authority by way of Basel II's recommendations to prescribe rapid remedial action for banks in such a situation.

**3) Pillar III- Market Discipline:**

Pillar III looks to increase market discipline within a country's banking sector. In sum, disclosures of a bank's capital and risk-taking positions that were once only available to regulators are recommended to be released to the general public in the Basel II Accord. Statistics such as the aggregate amounts of surplus capital (both Tier 1 and Tier 2) held by a bank, risk-weighted capital adequacy ratios, reserve requirements for credit, market, and operational risk, and a full description (with assumptions) of the risk mitigation approaches of a bank are recommended for quarterly release to the general public under Basel II's standards. With this action, Basel II hopes to empower shareholders to enforce discipline in the risk-taking and reserve-holding methods of banks, where banks seem to hold too few reserves and take on too much risk are punished by their own shareholders for doing so.

## 3.5.3 Basel - III:

Basel III is an extension of the existing Basel II Framework, and introduces new capital and liquidity standards to strengthen the regulation, supervision, and risk management of the whole of the banking and finance sector.

It was agreed upon by the members of the Basel Committee on Banking Supervision in 2010–2011, and was scheduled to be introduced from 2013 until 2015. However, changes made from April 2013 extended implementation until March 31, 2018. The Basel III requirements were in response to the deficiencies in financial regulation that is revealed by the 2000's financial crisis. Basel III was intended to strengthen bank capital requirements by increasing bank liquidity and decreasing bank leverage.

The global capital framework and new capital buffers require financial institutions to hold more capital and higher quality of capital than under current Basel II rules. The new leverage ratio introduces a no risk-based measure to supplement the risk-based minimum capital requirements. The new liquidity ratios ensure that adequate funding is maintained in case there are other severe banking crises.

**A) Capital Requirements:**

The Basel III rule introduced the following measures to strengthen the capital requirement and introduced more capital buffers:

**1) Capital Conservation Buffer:**

Capital Conservation Buffer is designed to absorb losses during periods of financial and economic stress. Financial institutions will be required to hold a capital conservation buffer of 2.5% to withstand future periods of stress, bringing the total common equity requirement to 7% (4.5% common equity requirement and the 2.5% capital conservation buffer). The capital conservation buffer must be met exclusively with common equity. Financial institutions that do not maintain the capital conservation buffer faces restrictions on payouts of dividends, share buybacks, and bonuses.

**2) Countercyclical Capital Buffer:**

Countercyclical Capital Buffer is a countercyclical buffer within a range of 0% and 2.5% of common equity or other fully loss absorbing capital is implemented according to national circumstances. This buffer serves as an extension to the capital conservation buffer.

**3) Higher Common Equity Tier (CET 1):**

Higher Common Equity Tier 1 (CET1) constitutes an increase from 2% to 4.5%. The ratio is set at:

a) 3.5% from 1 January 2013
b) 4% from 1 January 2014
c) 4.5% from 1 January 2015

**4) Minimum Total Capital ratio:**

Minimum Total Capital Ratio remains at 8%. The addition of the capital conservation buffer increases the total amount of capital a financial institution must hold to 10.5% of risk-weighted assets, of which 8.5% must be tier 1 capital. Tier 2 capital instruments are harmonized and tier 3 capital is abolished.

**B) Leverage Ratio:**

Basel III introduced a minimum "leverage ratio". The leverage ratio was calculated by dividing Tier 1 capital by the bank's average total consolidated assets; the banks were expected to maintain a leverage ratio in excess of 3% under Basel III. In July 2013, the US Federal Reserve Bank announced that the minimum Basel III leverage ratio would be 6% for 8 SIFI banks and 5% for their bank holding companies.

**C) Liquidity Requirements:**

Basel III introduced two required liquidity ratios:

**1) Liquidity Coverage Ratio (LCR) :**

Liquidity Coverage Ratio (LCR) ensures that sufficient levels of high-quality liquid assets are available for one-month survival in a severe stress scenario.

**2) Net Stable Funding Ratio (NSFR) :**

Net Stable Funding Ratio (NSFR) promotes resilience over long-term time horizons by creating more incentives for financial institutions to fund their activities with more stable sources of funding on an ongoing structural basis.

**D) Changes to Counterparty Credit Risk (CCR) :**

Basel III introduced capital requirements to cover Credit Value Adjustment (CVA) risk and higher capital requirements for securitization products

### 3.5.4 Basel - IV:

The Basel IV standards are changes to global bank capital requirements that were agreed in 2017 and are due for implementation in January 2023. They amend the international banking standards known as the Basel Accords. Regulators argue that these changes are simply completing the Basel III reforms, agreed in principle in 2010–11, although most of the Basel III reforms were agreed in detail at that time. The Basel Committee (BCBS) itself calls them simply "finalised reforms" and the UK Government has called them "Basel 3.1". Critics of the reform, in particular those from the banking industry, argue that Basel IV require a significant increase in capital and should be treated as a distinct round of reforms.

In December 2017 the Basel Committee on Banking Supervision (BCBS) published a package of proposed reforms for the global regulatory framework of our industry which is frequently referred to as 'Basel IV'. The Committee's aim is to make the capital framework more robust and to improve confidence in the system. Here, Dixit Joshi, Group Treasurer, and Steve Morris, Head of Group Finance, discuss the Basel IV framework in general, what happens next and potential implications for Deutsche Bank.

The Basel Committee on Banking Supervision or BCBS has proposed reforms which are designed to make banks more resilient and increase confidence in the banking system. The proposals announced recently, referred to as 'Basel IV', include updates to the ways banks calculate their capital requirements with the aim of making outcomes more comparable across banks globally.

1) **Purpose of Basel-IV:**

The Committee, headquartered at the Bank for International Settlements in Basel, was established to enhance financial stability by improving the quality of banking supervision worldwide, and to serve as a forum for regular cooperation between its member countries on banking supervisory matters.

2) **Importance of Basel-IV:**

Basel IV introduces changes that limit the reduction in capital that can result from banks' use of internal models under the Internal Ratings-Based approach. This includes:

a) A standardised floor, so that the capital requirement will always be at least 72.5% of the requirement under the Standardized approach

b) A simultaneous reduction in standardised risk weights for low risk mortgage loans;

c) A higher leverage ratio for Global Systemically Important Banks (G-SIBs), with the increase equal to 50% of the risk adjusted capital ratio

d) More detailed disclosure of reserves and other financial statistics.

These reforms will take effect from January 2023 (with exception of the output floor, which is phased in, taking full effect only on 1 January 2027).

British banks alone may have to raise another £50Bn in capital in order to meet Basel IV requirements. The average Common Equity Tier 1 (CET1) capital ratio for major European banks is estimated to fall by 0.9%, with the biggest impact on banks in Sweden and Denmark of 2.5%–3%.

✶✶✶✶✶✶✶

## Review Questions

**Q.1 Answers in 100 Words:**

1) Explain the Meaning of Banking Sector Reforms.
2) Discuss the Goals of Banking Sector Reforms in India.
3) Explain the Establishment and Scope of Narsimhan Committee - I.
4) State the Concept of Basel- I.
5) Write Short Note on Basel- IV.

**Q.2 Answers in 200 Words:**

1) Explain the Recommendations of the Narsimhan Committee - I.
2) Discuss about the Income Recognition and Asset Classification.
3) State the Cash Reserve Ratio (C.R.R.) and Statutory Liquidity Ratio (S.L.R).
4) Discuss about the Basel - III.

**Q.3 Answers in 300 Words:**

1) Explain the Meaning and Goals of Banking Sector Reforms.
2) Discuss the Reforms of Narsimhan Committee - I.
3) Explain the Recommendations of the Narsimhan Committee - II.
4) Discuss in detail about the Basel - II.

**Q.4 Write Short Note on Following:**

1) Cash Reserve Ratio.
2) Statutory Liquidity Ratio.
3) Prudential Norms.
4) Non-Performing Assets (NPAs).
5) Capital Adequacy Norms/ Ratio.
6) Credit Deposit Ratio (C. D. Ratio).
7) Basel- I.

✶✶✶✶✶✶✶

UNIT 4

# Innovative Banking in India

**4.1 MUDRA Scheme**

**4.2 Small Finance Banks**

**4.3 Payment Banks**

**4.4 Bandhan Bank**

## Introduction:

Innovation means something new or something which had not been done before. The same goes for banking section as well. There are many sections in banks which are going through or have gone through innovation in recent past. They are no longer restricted to age-old (traditional) methods. Thus, to increase the business avenues and capture the new market banks are resorting to innovation. This term innovative banking is being in use a lot nowadays. The banking sector is constantly evolving, new technology is continuously being introduced into banking systems and leaders in the banking industry are continuing to implement ground-breaking financial products and services. There has been strategic investment in recent banking innovations through crowdsourcing, piloting, collaborations and partnering to develop revolutionary banking solutions. With the ever-changing banking sector new regulations and revised banking standards have been developed. Digital-only banking is perhaps the most significant change that has happened in the financial industry in the last few years.

## 4.1 MUDRA Scheme:

Pradhan Mantri MUDRA Yojana (PMMY) is a scheme launched by the Hon'ble Prime Minister on April 8, 2015 for providing loans upto 10 lakh to the non-corporate, non-farm small/micro enterprises. These loans are classified as MUDRA loans under PMMY. These loans are given by Commercial Banks, RRBs, Small Finance Banks, Cooperative Banks, MFIs and NBFCs. The borrower can approach any of the lending institutions mentioned above or can apply online through this portal. Under the aegis of PMMY,

MUDRA has created three products namely 'Shishu', 'Kishore' and 'Tarun' to signify the stage of growth and funding needs of the beneficiary micro unit/entrepreneur and also provide a reference point for the next phase of graduation/growth.

**A) Eligibility of the Borrower:**

Loans would be provided to all the non-farm income-generating businesses in trading, manufacturing and services whose credit requirements are less than Rs.10 lakhs by all Public Sector Banks, State Cooperative Banks, Regional Rural Banks and Urban Co-operative Banks would be known as Mudra loans under the PMMY (Pradhan Mantri Mudra Yojana). Basically, all those who want to avail loans below Rs.10 lakhs for micro units are qualified for such loan. An application form under the scheme would be available with each of the above-mentioned institutions. This application form needs to be submitted together with the documents listed below:

**1)** Proof of Identity
**2)** Identity Proof/Address Proof of the Business (relevant certificates & licenses).
**3)** Category Proof, if any.
**4)** Statement of accounts for the last six months.
**5)** Income Tax Returns along with last two years balance sheet.
**6)** Proof business existence, such as Memorandum of Association or Partnership Deed.

Apart from the documents mentioned above, applicants' banks might ask for other documents as required. The Banks should not charge any processing fee and aren't supposed to request any collateral. The loan repayment period is extended to 5 years. However, it is made clear that any applicant shouldn't be a defaulter to any financial institution.

**B) Loan Limits and Interest Rates under Mudra Scheme:**

As per the choices for financing available under this scheme, the loan limits and interest rates vary for accommodating for the growth phase of the respective business availing such loan. The applicable limits and rates are as follows:

**1) Shishu:**

Loans up to a limit of Rs.50,000. The interest rate would depend on the bank, as per the guidelines of the schemes and keeping in view the applicant's credit history. Loan repayment period is dependent on the option of the bank.

**2) Kishore:**

Loans from Rs.50,000 up to Rs.5,00,00. The interest rate would depend on the bank, as per the guidelines of the schemes and keeping in view the applicant's credit history. Loan repayment period is dependent on the option of the bank.

**3) Tarun:**

Loans from Rs.5,00,000 up to Rs.10,00,000. The interest rate would depend on the bank, as per the guidelines of the schemes and keeping in view the applicant's credit history. Loan repayment period is dependent on the option of the bank.

Overall 27 Public Sector Banks, 31 Regional Rural Banks, 17 Private Sector Banks, 36 Microfinance Institutions, 25 Non-Banking Financial Institutions and 4 Co-operative banks have been selected for disbursing this loan as of now. 60 per cent of the loans under the scheme to be offered via 'Shishu' option and the remaining 40 per cent would be via 'Kishore' and 'Tarun' schemes.

**C) Sectors Covered:**

To maximize coverage of beneficiaries and tailor products to meet requirements of specific business activities, sector / activity focused schemes would be rolled out. To begin with, based on higher concentration of businesses in certain activities / sectors, schemes are proposed for:

1) **Land Transport Sector / Activity**:
Which will inter alia support units for purchase of transport vehicles for goods and personal transport such as auto rickshaw; small goods transport vehicle, 3 wheelers, e-rickshaw, passenger cars, taxis, etc.

2) **Community, Social & Personal Service Activities**:
Such as saloons, beauty parlours, gymnasium, boutiques, tailoring shops, dry cleaning, cycle and motorcycle repair shop, DTP and Photocopying Facilities, Medicine Shops, Courier Agents, etc.

3) **Food Products Sector**:
Support would be available for undertaking activities such as papad making, achaar making, jam / jelly making, agricultural produce preservation at rural level, sweet shops, small service food stalls and day to day catering / canteen services, cold chain vehicles, cold storages, ice making units, ice cream making units, biscuit, bread and bun making, etc.

4) **Textile Products Sector / Activity**:
To provide support for undertaking activities such as handloom, powerloom, chikan work, zari and zardozi work, traditional embroidery and hand work, traditional dyeing and printing, apparel design, knitting, cotton ginning, computerized embroidery, stitching and other textile non garment products such as bags, vehicle accessories, furnishing accessories, etc.

**D) Objectives of Pradhan Mantri Mudra Yojana:**

Following are the objectives of mudra loan scheme:

1) **Funding the Unfunded**:
To sanction loans up to rupees 10 Lakhs to those who have a business plan to generate income from a non-farm activity like manufacturing, processing, trading, or service sector but don't have enough capital to invest

2) **Reducing Jobless Economic Growth:**
To help generate sources of employment and increase the overall GDP by providing micro-enterprises with credit facilities.

**3) Monitoring and Regulating the Microfinance Institutions (MFI):**
With the help of MUDRA bank, the network of microfinance institutions will be monitored and new registration will also be done.

**4) Integration of Informal Economy into Formal Sector:**
It will help India also grow its tax base as incomes from the informal sector are non-taxed.

**5) Promoting Financial Inclusion:**
PMMY further adds to the vision of financial inclusion with the aim to reach the last mile credit delivery to micro-businesses and taking the help of technology solutions.

**E) Features of Mudra Yojana:**
The following are the main features of the MUDRA Yojana:

**1) Micro Credit Scheme:**
Under the Micro Credit Scheme, Micro Financial Institutions (MFIs) can obtain financing for enhancing their purchasing power for the qualifying assets. It's available for an individual or even a group of individuals who wants to set up a microenterprise.

**2) MUDRA Card:**
MUDRA card is a special product designed to make credit easily accessible and usable. A person can use a MUDRA card as a credit card for the overdraft limit. However, they can also use it as a debit card by withdrawing money from the ATMs.

**3) Credit Guarantee Fund Scheme:**
In a bid to reduce the credit risk for the lending institutions, the cabinet announced credit guarantee fund scheme under which it's expected to provide up to Rs. 1,00,000 crores worth of loans.

**4) Mahila Uddyami Scheme:**
As the name suggests, the Mahila Uddyami Scheme was specially designed for the welfare of the women. It helps women, self-help groups of women, and joint liability groups etc. to set up micro enterprises. All eligible women are provided special interest concessions under this scheme.

## 4.2 Small Finance Banks:

In India, where extending banking services to the underserved and unserved sections of the population is a challenge, there is merit in considering access to bank credit and services through expansion of small banks in unbanked and under-banked regions. In India an experiment with small banks was taken up following an announcement made by the then Finance Minister in the Union Budget in August 1996 and the RBI issued guidelines for setting up of Local Area Banks (LABs) vide its Press Release dated August 24, 1996. The LABs were conceived as low cost structures which would provide efficient and competitive financial intermediation services in a limited area of operation, i.e., primarily in rural and semi-urban areas. LABs were required to have a minimum capital of Rs. 5 crore and an area of operation comprising three contiguous districts. Presently, four LABs are functioning satisfactorily.

Taking into account the above and that small finance banks can play an important role in the supply of credit to micro and small enterprises, agriculture and banking services in unbanked and under-banked regions in the country, the RBI has decided to licence new "small finance banks" in the private sector. While permitting small banks, however, the issues relating to their size, capital requirements, area of operations, exposure norms, regulatory prescriptions, corporate governance and resolution need to be suitably addressed in the light of experience gained. Hence RBI has come out with following guidelines for licensing of small finance banks in the private sector.

### 4.2.1 Organisation of Small Finance Banks:

Small finance banks (SFBs) are a specialized type of bank in India that focuses on providing financial services to underserved and unbanked segments of the population. The organizational structure of SFBs is designed to enable them to achieve their objectives of promoting financial inclusion and providing basic banking services to these segments of the population. Here are the key components of the organizational structure of SFBs:

1) **Board of Directors:**
   The board of directors is responsible for the overall governance and strategic direction of the SFB. It is composed of independent directors and representatives from the promoter group, and it oversees the management team.
2) **Promoter Group:**
   The promoter group is the group of entities or individuals who promote the SFB and hold the majority shareholding. They play a critical role in the development of the SFB and provide strategic guidance.
3) **Chief Executive Officer:**
   The chief executive officer (CEO) is the top executive of the SFB and is responsible for the day-to-day operations of the bank. The CEO is appointed by the board of directors and oversees the management team.
4) **Management Team:**
   The management team is responsible for implementing the strategy and policies of the SFB. It includes executives in charge of functions such as finance, operations, technology, risk management, compliance, and human resources.
5) **Branch Network:**
   The SFB has a network of branches that are strategically located to serve customers in both urban and rural areas. The branches offer a range of banking services, including deposit-taking, lending, payment and remittance services, and bill payment services.

**6) Customer Service:**

SFBs place a strong emphasis on customer service and have dedicated customer service teams that are available to assist customers with their banking needs. These teams can be reached through various channels such as phone, email, and chat.

**7) Technology Infrastructure:**

SFBs rely heavily on technology to provide efficient and cost-effective banking services. They have robust technology infrastructure that includes core banking systems, mobile banking applications, internet banking portals, and other digital platforms.

**8) Compliance and Risk Management:**

SFBs are subject to strict regulatory requirements and have dedicated compliance and risk management teams that ensure that the bank operates within the regulatory framework and manages risks effectively.

**9) Partnerships:**

SFBs often partner with other financial institutions, technology companies, and service providers to expand their reach and offer a wider range of services to their customers.

**10) Investors:**

SFBs are typically backed by a diverse group of investors, including institutional investors, retail investors, and the promoter group.

**11) Business Correspondents:**

SFBs rely heavily on Business Correspondents (BCs) to reach out to unbanked and under banked customers in rural and semi-urban areas. BCs are local individuals or entities that act as an agent of the SFB and offer basic banking services such as deposit and withdrawal of cash, and loan disbursement and recovery.

**12) Credit Assessment:**

SFBs have specialized teams that focus on credit assessment of small and medium enterprises (SMEs), micro-enterprises, and other segments that are typically not served by larger banks. These teams are responsible for evaluating the creditworthiness of borrowers and ensuring that the loans are repaid on time.

### 4.2.2 Functions of Small Finance Banks:

Small finance banks (SFBs) are specialized banks that focus on providing financial services to underserved and unbanked segments of the population in India. They are licensed under the Banking Regulation Act, 1949, and are regulated by the Reserve Bank of India (RBI). The primary objective of SFBs is to promote financial inclusion by providing basic banking services such as deposits, loans, payment and remittance services, and insurance to these segments of the population. Here are the key functions of small finance banks:

**1) Acceptance of Deposits:**

SFBs are authorized to accept deposits from the public, subject to certain conditions set by the RBI. They offer various types of deposit accounts, including savings accounts, current accounts, fixed deposits, recurring deposits, and other deposit schemes.

**2) Lending:**

SFBs provide credit to small and medium-sized enterprises (SMEs), micro-enterprises, farmers, self-help groups, and other segments that are typically not served by larger banks. They offer a range of loan products, including agriculture loans, microfinance loans, personal loans, business loans, and housing loans.

**3) Payment and Remittance Services:**

SFBs offer payment and remittance services to their customers, including domestic and international money transfers, bill payments, mobile recharges, and other value-added services.

**4) Insurance:**

SFBs are permitted to act as corporate agents or brokers for the distribution of insurance products, including life, health, and general insurance. They also offer their own insurance products to their customers.

**5) Microfinance:**

SFBs are mandated to allocate at least 50% of their loan portfolio to microfinance, which involves lending to small and micro-enterprises, self-help groups, and other low-income households. They provide credit for income-generating activities such as agriculture, livestock, and small businesses.

**6) Financial Inclusion:**

SFBs play a critical role in promoting financial inclusion by providing basic banking services to underserved and unbanked segments of the population. They focus on reaching out to customers in rural and semi-urban areas by leveraging technology, partnerships, and business correspondents.

**7) Priority Sector Lending:**

SFBs are required to allocate at least 75% of their net bank credit to priority sectors such as agriculture, micro and small enterprises, education, and housing. This is aimed at promoting inclusive growth and development.

**8) Foreign Exchange Services:**

SFBs are authorized to provide foreign exchange services, including currency exchange, foreign currency accounts, and other related services.

**9) Digital Banking:**

SFBs leverage technology to offer digital banking services to their customers, including mobile banking, internet banking, and other digital platforms. They also offer biometric authentication and other advanced security features to ensure the safety and security of customer transactions.

**10) Financial Literacy and Education:**

SFBs play an important role in promoting financial literacy and education among their customers. They conduct financial literacy programs, workshops, and seminars to educate their customers about banking products and services, financial planning, and money management.

### 4.2.3 Importance of Small Finance Banks:

Small finance banks (SFBs) play a critical role in promoting financial inclusion and supporting the growth and development of underserved and unbanked segments of the population in India. Here are some key points that highlight the importance of SFBs:

**1) Financial Inclusion:**

SFBs are key players in promoting financial inclusion by providing basic banking services to segments of the population that have been traditionally excluded from the formal financial system. This includes low-income households, rural and semi-urban areas, and small and medium-sized enterprises (SMEs). By offering affordable and convenient banking services, SFBs help to increase access to financial services and promote financial literacy among underserved communities.

**2) Lending to Underserved Segments:**

SFBs focus on lending to underserved segments of the population, including micro and small enterprises, agriculture, and microfinance. This is important because these segments have limited access to credit from traditional banks and financial institutions. SFBs are able to provide customized loan products and services that meet the unique needs of these segments, thereby supporting their growth and development.

**3) Priority Sector Lending:**

SFBs are required to allocate at least 75% of their net bank credit to priority sectors such as agriculture, micro and small enterprises, education, and housing. This helps to support inclusive growth and development by channeling credit to sectors that are critical for the overall development of the economy.

**4) Job Creation:**

By providing credit to SMEs and micro-enterprises, SFBs help to support job creation and entrepreneurship. SMEs are the backbone of the Indian economy, and access to credit is critical for their growth and development. SFBs help to fill this gap by providing customized loan products and services that meet the unique needs of SMEs and micro-enterprises.

**5) Rural Development:**

SFBs play an important role in promoting rural development by providing banking services to rural areas. This helps to promote financial inclusion and supports the growth and development of agriculture, which is a critical sector for the Indian economy. By providing credit to farmers and other rural enterprises, SFBs help to support the growth and development of rural areas.

6) **Microfinance:**
SFBs are required to allocate at least 50% of their loan portfolio to microfinance. This involves lending to small and micro-enterprises, self-help groups, and other low-income households. By providing credit for income-generating activities such as agriculture, livestock, and small businesses, SFBs help to support the growth and development of these segments, thereby promoting financial inclusion and supporting economic growth.

7) **Digital Banking:**
SFBs leverage technology to offer digital banking services to their customers, including mobile banking, internet banking, and other digital platforms. This helps to increase access to banking services, particularly in remote and rural areas, where physical banking infrastructure is limited. By providing cost-effective and convenient banking services, SFBs help to promote financial inclusion and support the growth and development of underserved segments of the population.

8) **Competition and Innovation:**
SFBs are relatively new players in the Indian banking industry, and their entry has increased competition and innovation in the sector. This has led to the development of new products and services, as well as improvements in customer service and banking infrastructure. By promoting competition and innovation, SFBs help to improve the overall quality of banking services in the country.

## 4.3 Payment Banks:

Payments banks are new model of banks, conceptualised by the Reserve Bank of India (RBI), which cannot issue credit. These banks can accept a restricted deposit, which is currently limited to ₹200,000 per customer and may be increased further. These banks cannot issue loans and credit cards. Both current account and savings accounts can be operated by such banks. Payments banks can issue ATM cards or debit cards and provide online or mobile banking. Bharti Airtel set up India's first payments bank, Airtel Payments Bank.

### 4.3.1 Organisation of Payment Banks:

The organizational structure of payment banks is designed to enable them to achieve their objectives of promoting financial inclusion and providing basic banking services to underserved and unbanked segments of the population. Here are the key components of the organizational structure of payment banks:

1) **Board of Directors:**
The board of directors is responsible for the overall governance and strategic direction of the payment bank. It is composed of independent directors and representatives from the promoter group, and it oversees the management team.

**2) Promoter Group:**

The promoter group is the group of entities or individuals who promote the payment bank and hold the majority shareholding. They play a critical role in the development of the payment bank and provide strategic guidance.

**3) Chief Executive Officer:**

The chief executive officer (CEO) is the top executive of the payment bank and is responsible for the day-to-day operations of the bank. The CEO is appointed by the board of directors and oversees the management team.

**4) Management Team:**

The management team is responsible for implementing the strategy and policies of the payment bank. It includes executives in charge of functions such as finance, operations, technology, risk management, compliance, and human resources.

**5) Branch Network:**

The payment bank has a network of branches that are strategically located to serve customers in both urban and rural areas. The branches offer a range of banking services, including deposit-taking, payment and remittance services, and bill payment services.

**6) Customer Service:**

Payment banks place a strong emphasis on customer service and have dedicated customer service teams that are available to assist customers with their banking needs. These teams can be reached through various channels such as phone, email, and chat.

**7) Technology Infrastructure:**

Payment banks rely heavily on technology to provide efficient and cost-effective banking services. They have robust technology infrastructure that includes core banking systems, mobile banking applications, internet banking portals, and other digital platforms.

**8) Compliance and Risk Management:**

Payment banks are subject to strict regulatory requirements and have dedicated compliance and risk management teams that ensure that the bank operates within the regulatory framework and manages risks effectively.

**9) Partnerships:**

Payment banks often partner with other financial institutions, technology companies, and service providers to expand their reach and offer a wider range of services to their customers.

**10) Investors:**

Payment banks are typically backed by a diverse group of investors, including institutional investors, retail investors, and the promoter group

### 4.3.2 Functions of Payment Banks:

Payment banks are a new category of banks that have been introduced in some countries to promote financial inclusion and provide basic banking services to a large number of people who are unbanked or under banked. These banks are licensed by the central bank and are subject to specific regulatory requirements that are different from traditional banks. Here are some of the key functions of payment banks:

1) **Deposit-taking:**
   Payment banks can accept deposits from individuals and small businesses, subject to a limit of INR 2 lakhs per account. They can offer savings accounts, current accounts, and recurring deposit accounts.
2) **Payment and Remittance Services:**
   Payment banks offer payment and remittance services to their customers, enabling them to send and receive money domestically and internationally. They have a wide range of payment channels such as mobile banking, internet banking, and ATM services.
3) **Digital Banking Services:**
   Payment banks offer digital banking services to their customers, allowing them to access their accounts, make transactions, and manage their finances online or through mobile applications.
4) **Prepaid Payment Instruments:**
   Payment banks can issue prepaid payment instruments such as prepaid debit cards, digital wallets, and prepaid gift cards, which can be used for various transactions and purchases.
5) **Bill Payment Services:**
   Payment banks provide bill payment services to their customers, allowing them to pay their utility bills, mobile bills, and other bills electronically.
6) **Financial Products:**
   Payment banks can offer various financial products such as mutual funds, insurance products, and pension products in partnership with other financial institutions.
7) **Small Business Banking Services:**
   Payment banks offer banking services to small businesses, enabling them to manage their finances, make transactions, and access credit products.
8) **Money Market Operations:**
   Payment banks can participate in the money market operations of the central bank and invest in short-term government securities.
9) **Financial Literacy:**
   Payment banks can promote financial literacy among their customers by offering educational materials and financial advisory services. This helps customers to better manage their finances and make informed financial decisions.

**10) KYC Services:**

Payment banks can offer KYC (Know Your Customer) services to other financial institutions, enabling them to comply with regulatory requirements and verify the identity of their customers.

**11) Foreign Exchange Services:**

Payment banks can offer foreign exchange services such as currency exchange, forex cards, and remittance services for international payments.

**12) Agency Banking:**

Payment banks can act as agents for other banks and financial institutions, enabling them to reach out to customers in remote areas and expand their reach.

### 4.3.3 Importance of Payment Banks:

Payment banks are a unique type of financial institution that offer limited banking services to a specific demographic of individuals and businesses. They have gained importance in recent years, particularly in emerging markets, where they are helping to promote financial inclusion and bridge the gap between traditional banking services and the unbanked population. Here are some of the key reasons why payment banks are important:

**1) Promote Financial Inclusion:**

One of the most significant benefits of payment banks is that they help to promote financial inclusion. In many emerging markets, a significant portion of the population remains unbanked, either because they do not have access to traditional banking services or because they cannot afford them. Payment banks, with their low fees, simplified account opening procedures, and digital banking capabilities, are helping to bring banking services to these underserved populations.

**2) Facilitate Digital Payments:**

Payment banks are at the forefront of facilitating digital payments, which are increasingly becoming the norm in many countries. They offer various payment channels, such as mobile banking, internet banking, and ATMs, to facilitate transactions, which are faster, cheaper, and more convenient than traditional payment methods. By promoting digital payments, payment banks are also helping to reduce the usage of cash, which can help to reduce the risks of fraud and theft.

**3) Provide Basic Banking Services:**

Payment banks offer basic banking services, such as savings accounts, current accounts, and remittance services, to individuals and small businesses. These services are essential to manage finances, facilitate business transactions, and build a credit history, which is critical for accessing credit in the future.

**4) Promote Entrepreneurship and Economic Growth:**

Payment banks are helping to promote entrepreneurship and economic growth by providing basic banking services to small businesses, which are often overlooked by traditional banks. By providing these services, payment banks are helping to facilitate the growth of small businesses, which are a critical engine for economic growth and job creation.

5) **Foster Financial Literacy:**

Payment banks are also helping to foster financial literacy by educating their customers about basic financial concepts and helping them to manage their finances effectively. This education can help customers make informed financial decisions and avoid costly mistakes that can lead to financial difficulties.

6) **Reduce Transaction Costs:**

Payment banks offer low transaction costs for their services, which makes them attractive to low-income populations who are sensitive to transaction costs. This can help to reduce the overall cost of transactions for customers and make banking services more accessible to low-income populations.

7) **Increase Competition in the Banking Sector:**

Payment banks have increased competition in the banking sector by offering innovative and affordable services to customers. This competition is forcing traditional banks to improve their services and reduce their fees, which benefits customers.

8) **Enhance Financial Stability:**

Payment banks are regulated by the central bank, which helps to ensure that they operate within the confines of the law and adhere to sound banking practices. This regulation helps to enhance financial stability by reducing the risks of bank failures and systemic risks to the financial system.

In conclusion, payment banks are an essential tool in promoting financial inclusion and economic growth in emerging markets. They offer basic banking services to underserved populations, facilitate digital payments, promote entrepreneurship, foster financial literacy, reduce transaction costs, increase competition in the banking sector, and enhance financial stability. As such, payment banks play a critical role in building a more inclusive and robust financial system that benefits all members of society.

## 4.4 Bandhan Bank:

Bandhan Bank Ltd. is a banking and financial services company, headquartered in Kolkata. Bandhan Bank is present in 34 out of 36 states and union territories of India, with 5,723 banking outlets and more than 2.86 crore customers. Having received the universal banking licence from the Reserve Bank of India, Bandhan Bank started operations on August 23, 2015, with 501 branches, 50 ATMs and 2,022 Banking Units (BUs). The Bank has mobilised deposits of over ₹1,02,283 crore and its total advances stand at over ₹97,787 crore as of December 31, 2022.

**1) History:**

Bandhan was set up in 2001 as a not-for-profit entity with the objective of financial inclusion and women empowerment through sustainable livelihood creation. It started its microfinance operations from Bagnan, a small village, about 60 km from Kolkata. The model followed for delivery of microfinance services was individual lending through group formation. Bandhan focused on serving underbanked and underpenetrated markets.

In 2006, Bandhan acquired a Non-Banking Financial Company (NBFC) and created Bandhan Financial Services Private Limited (BFSPL) to scale up its microfinance activities. In 2010, it became the largest microfinance institution (MFI) in the country. In April 2014, Bandhan received an in-principle approval from the Reserve Bank of India (RBI). On June 17, 2015, RBI granted the banking licence to Bandhan, making it the first-ever microfinance institution to become a universal bank in India. Bandhan Bank commenced operations on August 23, 2015. The then Union Finance Minister, Late Shri Arun Jaitley, inaugurated the Bank in Kolkata. Its public shareholders then included International Finance Corporation; Caladium Investment Pte Ltd (the sovereign wealth fund of Singapore, an arm of GIC); and Small Industries Development Bank of India (SIDBI).

On 27 March 2018, Bandhan Bank was listed on the bourses and became the $8^{th}$ largest bank in India by market capital, on the day of listing itself.

**2) Operations:**

Bandhan Bank through its network of 5,639 banking outlets is spread across metro, urban, semi-urban and rural India. The key focus areas are micro-entrepreneurs, MSME segment, housing finance and retail assets. It is interesting to note that 84.5% of the Bank's deposits are in the retail segment, thus, granular in nature. Bandhan Bank is focused on inclusive banking and reaches out to the unbanked and under-banked segments of the country, with 73% of its branches situated in rural and semi-urban areas.

**3) Products and Services:**

The Bank's products and services ranges from savings to current accounts, from fixed deposits to credit cards, from home loans to personal loans, from insurance to mutual funds, and more.

**4) Merger:**

In October 2019, Bandhan Bank acquired GRUH Finance Limited; a Housing Development Finance Corporation Limited backed housing finance company in the share-swap deal by way of scheme of amalgamation, in order to venture into the affordable housing finance.

**5) Investors:**

Bandhan Bank is an associate of Bandhan Financial Holdings Limited (BFHL) which is holding 39.99% of stake in the Bank as on December 31, 2021. Further, BFHL is a wholly owned subsidiary of Bandhan Financial Services Limited (BFSL). Other major shareholders of the Bank as on December 31, 2021, are Housing Development Finance Corporation Limited (9.89%) and Caladium Investment Pte. Limited (7.79%).

**6) Listing and Shareholding:**

The equity shares of Bandhan Bank are listed on the BSE Limited and the National Stock Exchange of India Limited. The IPO of the Bank oversubscribed by almost 15 times at the end of the three-day long issue. On its stock exchange debut (March 27, 2018), the equity opened at ₹487.33 on the National Stock Exchange and closed at ₹476.85; 27% over its issue price of ₹375.

| Shareholders as on March 31, 2022 | Shareholding (%) |
|---|---|
| Promoter & Promoter Group* (BFHL) | 39.99 |
| Foreign Portfolio Investor (FPI) | 34.31 |
| Bodies Corporate | 9.71 |
| Individual Shareholders | 6.16 |
| Qualified Institutional Buyers | 3.91 |
| Others | 5.92 |

**7) Functions of Bandhan Bank:**

As a private sector bank in India, Bandhan Bank performs a variety of functions to meet the financial needs of its customers. Some of the key functions of Bandhan Bank include:

**a) Accepting Deposits:**

Bandhan Bank accepts deposits from its customers in the form of savings accounts, current accounts, and fixed deposits.

**b) Providing Loans:**

Bandhan Bank provides various types of loans to its customers, including personal loans, home loans, business loans, and agricultural loans.

**c) Issuing Credit Cards:**

Bandhan Bank issues credit cards to eligible customers, which can be used for making purchases and payments.

**d) Offering Investment Products:**

Bandhan Bank offers a range of investment products, such as mutual funds, insurance, and other wealth management products.

**e) Providing Digital Banking Services:**

Bandhan Bank offers digital banking services such as internet banking, mobile banking, and phone banking, which allows customers to access their accounts and perform various transactions remotely.

**f) Providing Financial Inclusion Services:**

Bandhan Bank is committed to promoting financial inclusion and providing banking services to under-served and under-banked communities in India. The bank has set up banking outlets in rural and semi-urban areas of the country to reach out to such communities.

**g) Providing other Banking Services:**

In addition to the above services, Bandhan Bank also provides other banking services such as remittance services, foreign exchange services, and ATM services.

**8) Importance of Bandhan Bank:**

Bandhan Bank plays an important role in the Indian banking sector and the overall financial landscape of the country. Here are some of the reasons why Bandhan Bank is considered important:

**a) Financial Inclusion:**

Bandhan Bank's focus on providing financial services to under-served and under-banked customers, particularly in rural and semi-urban areas, is a crucial step towards promoting financial inclusion in India. The bank has helped millions of people access banking services and participates in the formal economy.

**b) Job Creation:**

Since its inception as a microfinance company, Bandhan Bank has created thousands of jobs in India. The bank employs over 41,000 people and has also created indirect employment opportunities through its network of branches and banking outlets.

**c) SME and Micro-Enterprise Lending:**

Bandhan Bank has been instrumental in providing credit to small and medium-sized enterprises (SMEs) and micro-enterprises in India. By providing loans to these businesses, Bandhan Bank has supported job creation, economic growth, and entrepreneurship in the country.

**d) Digital Banking:**

Bandhan Bank has been at the forefront of digital banking in India, providing its customers with access to a range of digital banking services such as internet banking, mobile banking, and phone banking. This has made banking more convenient and accessible for customers, particularly those in remote areas.

**e) Social Impact:**

Bandhan Bank has received several awards and recognitions for its contribution to social impact and financial inclusion. The bank's efforts have helped reduce poverty, promote economic growth, and improve the standard of living for millions of people in India.

*******

## Review Questions

**Q.1 Answers in 100 Words:**

1) Explain the Objectives of MUDRA Scheme.
2) Explain the Functions of Small Finance Bank.
3) State the Organisational Structure of Payment Banks.
4) State the Importance of Bandhan Bank.

**Q.2 Answers in 200 Words:**

1) Explain the Features of MUDRA Scheme.
2) Discuss the Organisational Structure of Small Finance Bank.
3) Explain the Importance of Payment Banks.
4) Explain the Functions of Bandhan Bank.

**Q.3 Answers in 300 Words:**

1) Discuss in in detail about the MUDRA Scheme.
2) Explain the Functions and Importance of Small Finance Bank.
3) Discuss in detail Organisation and Functions of Payment Bank.
4) Write in detail about the Bandhan Bank.

**Q.4 Write Short Note on Following:**

1) MUDRA Scheme.
2) Small Finance Bank.
3) Payment Banks.
4) Bandhan Bank.

*******